RODNEY CLINE CAREW

MINNESOTA, A.L., 1967-1978
CALIFORNIA, A.L., 1979-1985

BATTING WIZARD WHO LINED, CHOPPED AND
BUNTED HIS WAY TO 3,053 HITS. 7 BATTING TITLES
SURPASSED ONLY BY COBB AND WAGNER. USED
VARIETY OF RELAXED, CROUCHED BATTING STANCES
TO HIT OVER .300 15 CONSECUTIVE SEASONS,
ACHIEVING .328 LIFETIME. A.L. ROOKIE OF YEAR
IN 1967 AND A.L. MVP 10 YEARS LATER WHEN HE
BATTED .388 WITH 239 HITS. NAMED TO 18 STRAIGHT
ALL-STAR TEAMS. NATIONAL HERO IN PANAMA.

Rod Carew's
HIT to WIN

Batting Tips and Techniques
from a Baseball Hall of Famer

WITH FRANK PACE AND ARMEN KETEYIAN   FOREWORD BY JOE MAUER

MVP
BOOKS

Published in 2012 by MVP Books, an imprint of MBI Publishing Company and the Quayside Publishing
Group, 400 First Avenue North, Suite 300, Minneapolis, MN 55401 USA

First edition published in 1986 as *Rod Carew's Art and Science of Hitting* by Viking Penguin Inc.

MVP Books titles are also available at discounts in bulk quantity for industrial or sales-promotional
use. For details write to Special Sales Manager at Quayside Publishing Group, 400 First Avenue
North, Suite 300, Minneapolis, MN 55401 USA.

To find out more about our books, visit us online at www.mvpbooks.com.

ISBN-13: 978-0-7603-4266-4

Carew, Rod, 1945-
 Rod Carew's hit to win : batting tips and techniques from a baseball hall of famer / Rod Carew; with
Frank Pace and Armen Keteyian; foreword by Joe Mauer.
    p. cm.
 ISBN 978-0-7603-4266-4 (flexibound)
 1. Batting (Baseball) I. Pace, Frank. II. Keteyian, Armen. III. Title. IV. Title: The art and science
of hitting.
 GV869.C365 2012
 796.357'26--dc23
                              2011041183

Editor: Adam Brunner
Design Manager: James Kegley
Designer: Simon Larkin
Illustrations: Matt Sagehorn
Front cover photo credit: Rich Pilling/MLB Photos via Getty Images

Printed in China

10 9 8 7 6 5 4 3 2 1

To Michelle

Contents

Foreword

By Joe Mauer

There might be no one more qualified to write a book about hitting than Rod Carew. And I know from experience.

Now, please understand that I was never able to see Rod play in person. When I was born in 1983, he was putting the finishing touches on a Hall of Fame career that included 3,053 hits, 7 batting titles, and 18 All-Star Game selections.

Most of what I've learned about Rod has come from my friendship with him, a friendship that has developed during his appearances in the Twin Cities and from his annual trips to Twins spring training in Fort Myers, where he suits up as a special coach.

He is special, indeed.

I've been privileged to listen to him talk about hitting while hanging around the batting cages, and I seek him out for information as much as I can—Rod has such a vast knowledge of the physical and mental aspects of hitting. As you move through the minors and reach the big leagues, you gain a greater understanding of the importance of the mental side of hitting.

What really stands out to me about Rod is how he *prepared* to be a good hitter. That's preparation in the batting cage and preparation to face specific pitchers and handle every situation at the plate.

I've definitely talked to him about having a routine, having a plan when I go to the plate. We've talked about what great hitters try to do in certain situations and about different opponents we've faced on the mound. You play so many games throughout the season, and if you're having success you try to hold on to it as long as you can. Rod was one of the most consistent hitters ever to play the game. He is someone we all strive to be.

He's pretty unbelievable and a great guy on top of that.

If you ask any current big-leaguer about Rod Carew, they will speak about him with total respect because of his accomplishments and the way he's carried himself with class through the years.

When Rod appears at the batting cage before games, players from both teams will approach him, shake his hand, and talk hitting.

Two of the Twins' best hitters talk shop in the dugout. *Hannah Foslien/Getty Images*

I believe Rod could have hit more home runs if he'd wanted to, but he sacrificed some power for high average. That's why I enjoy talking to him about hitting, because our principles are similar. If you can hit home runs and maintain a high average, that's great. But getting on base and working the counts on pitchers is an important part of the game that has been overlooked the past few years. And there were few better at that than Rod.

It's an honor for me to be able to talk to Rod about hitting. By reading this book, you will learn a lot of the things I've learned from him through the years. For you young hitters out there, this will be a tremendous resource for you as you work on your game. You'll learn about the importance of hitting the ball where it's pitched instead of trying to pull that low, outside pitch. You'll come to understand the importance of using your hands. And, something that's crucial for every hitter, you'll learn how to be confident at the plate. These are just a few examples of Rod's vast knowledge of hitting.

With the help of this book, you'll learn important things about yourself as a hitter as you identify your strengths and weaknesses. Rod Carew's insight will be something you can refer to time and again as you grow as a player and perfect your swing.

I've won three batting titles, and I still strive for the kind of success Rod had. He's one of the best pure hitters to ever play this game. I remember when, after I won my second batting title in 2008, Rod came up to me and said, "After you win a couple more, we'll take a picture with all our silver bats." I've won one more batting title since then, so I'm still a little short. It's hard enough to win just one, but I have a good reason to keep striving for more.

Rod, I'm looking forward to the day when we can take that picture.

Introduction & Philosophy

This is me back in the day—I was a pretty good hitter. In 1977 I almost hit .400, finishing the season at .388. I won my seventh American League batting title that year and was named A.L. Most Valuable Player. *Author's collection*

I loved to hit. I always did. Although it's fun, becoming a good hitter isn't always easy. I always get a good laugh every time I hear someone say, "Rod Carew was a born hitter; no one could hit like he did." Well, you may not win seven batting titles, but you can become a good hitter, a great hitter, if you want to work at it. I was a sickly child, not born to be a great athlete or to overpower any pitcher, but I worked and worked to draw as much out of my natural ability as I possibly could. I studied the game and paid my dues on countless dusty sandlot fields in Panama and later in the United States. I never stopped thinking, dreaming about becoming a great hitter. And I challenged myself. No matter how well I hit, how high my average rose, there was—and still is—a little voice inside me saying, "You can do better, Carew . . . you can do better."

Constantly striving to improve is important, but it is important at the start to understand *how* to improve, to grasp the essentials of good hitting. First and foremost, good hitting is doing whatever it takes to help your team win ballgames. That is why you go to the plate—to help your team win. Hitting is personal in the sense that only you can do it for yourself, but it is primarily a function of a team game. The more hits you can get, the more times you'll be on base to score runs and the more runs you'll drive in. That's obvious. But that's only one aspect of being a good hitter. A good hitter is also an unselfish hitter, one willing to move a runner over, to give himself up, to do the little things that don't always show up in the box score but still have a major impact on the outcome of the game.

It's no coincidence that some of the greatest hitters who have ever played the game were unselfish players. Frank Robinson, Hank Aaron, Pete Rose, and Derek Jeter all realized what it took to win ballgames. They never gave a moment's thought to making an out if it would advance a runner into scoring position, or to laying down a bunt when the situation called for it. Great hitters know a team's winning percentage is more important than any one player's batting average. So should you. Yet selflessness and desire are only two parts of the equation. Without equal portions of discipline and confidence, you're not going to be a threat at the plate. The late Charley Lau, hitting instructor for the Royals, Yankees, and White Sox, once wrote, "Rod Carew simply makes solid contact with the ball more often than other

This is me with my statue. That's right, the Twins thought I was good enough to deserve a statue in front of their beautiful new Target Field, along with Hall of Famers Harmon Killebrew and Kirby Puckett, and my old roomie Tony Oliva. I played 12 seasons with the Twins and hit .334 during my years in Minnesota. I spent the last seven years of my career with the Angels, where in 1985 I collected my 3,000th base hit. When I hung up my cleats both the Angels and Twins retired my uniform #29. *Jim Mone/AP Photo*

This is where I have worked for the past 50-plus years: on lush fields of green in front of mostly adoring fans. I have been blessed with the talent to hit a baseball as well as the ability to teach others to hit.

hitters." But consistent contact doesn't just happen. It comes from knowing the fundamentals of good hitting and applying them in a disciplined, confident manner. I know what works best for Rod Carew. I know what pitches I like to hit, what pitches I can—and cannot—hit, and where I want to hit every pitch I see. Consequently, I try never to stray from this philosophy, to mess with success. Yet the little laws that established—and now direct—that discipline didn't materialize overnight. It took me years and years of experimentation and self-analysis to decide what was right for me. As someone striving to become—or remain—a .300 hitter, realize you have to make a commitment. Hitting .300 is almost like a cause, a campaign. You can never really rest. You must always strive to learn more about your opponents, to outthink them, to outwork them. In the long run it can only add to your success, but before making this commitment, you must decide what hitting philosophy you will follow.

Over the years, hundreds of different styles, methods, and theories of how to hit a baseball have developed, but, unfortunately, some instructors remain limited in their knowledge. One may preach strictly "top hand, top hand"—a reference to rolling the top hand over as the barrel of the bat makes contact with the ball—and nothing else. One may preach weight back; another, weight forward; still another, hitting the ball back up the middle. The problem with these theories is that the people who have put them forth speak in absolutes, as if their way is the only way to hit.

This book will occasionally speak in absolutes, but it will not, under any circumstance, stress *one* absolute way, a single concept, of hitting a baseball. Hitting is a multidimensional process. You can learn a little bit from a lot of people. What this book will do is stress the importance of fundamentals and experimentation and the fact that every hitter is unique. I won't say "hit like me or else." I don't believe there is any one path to hitting excellence, and it's finally time for me to say so. You only have to look at the disparate styles of a Lance Berkman, who hits from a more crouched stance, and a Kevin Youkilis, who stands upright at the plate, to understand that.

When I played in Major League Baseball, Tony Gwynn, Wade Boggs, and George Brett shared a similar approach to hitting, even though our mechanics differed. Today I would say the same thing about Ichiro Suzuki of the Seattle Mariners, Robinson Canó of the New York Yankees, and Albert Pujols. Each is different from the others and from me in many ways, but all are similar in their approach to spraying the ball to all fields.

This is a batter's box. It used to be my office. Now it's my classroom. I once heard a fan ask a Hall of Famer, "How did you get to Cooperstown?" The answer was a humorous "practice, practice, practice." Well that's close to the truth, but practice doesn't make perfect; perfect practice makes perfect. Perfect practice is at the heart of what I will be teaching in this book.

The pitcher is the enemy, and he lives just 60 feet and 6 inches from the batter's box. He can be a formidable foe, but this book will teach you how to exploit him to your advantage.

Pujols is seen by many as the best player in baseball over the last 10 years, and though he hits for power, he still uses the entire field. His stance sees him crouch more than most hitters these days, but he uses his whole body and is balanced throughout his swing. Suzuki, an American League all-star regular, is a consummate contact hitter and, like me in many ways, he is a hands hitter. He uses extraordinary hand speed to wait for a pitch to get deep in the zone before turning on it. Canó, a World Series champion who is emerging as the best second baseman in baseball, takes a similar approach to me in using his legs to stay on the same plane as the pitch.

Ted Williams was certainly a great hitter, one of the greatest of all time, and a fine hitting coach, but I don't agree with everything Ted said about hitting. Ted stressed knowledge of the strike zone, linking batting average to the location of the pitches you swing at. I don't believe in this approach. I believe it's more important to know what pitches you can hit and where to hit those pitches.

This is the pitcher's weapon, the baseball. It's a cork center, covered with yarn, covered with cowhide and sewn together with 108 double stitches. It can be thrown at speeds of up to 100 miles an hour and made to rise, curve, dip, or float like a butterfly.

These are our weapons: soft hands wielding 31 to 36 ounces of a finely engineered bat. It's been said that the hardest thing to do in sports is to take a round bat and hit a round ball squarely. Our goal in this book is to make that task a little easier.

To me, knowledge of your *own* hitting zone is more important than knowledge of *the* strike zone. I'm not going to swing at every pitch that arrives between the armpits and the knees just because it's a strike. I'd much rather take a called strike than swing at a pitch I'm not prepared to handle.

So, ultimately, my message is this: I couldn't hit like Ted Williams any more than you can hit like me. But we can share basic fundamentals and philosophies of hitting in our quest to get the most out of our talents. You'll learn my philosophies, my fundamentals, in this book. But, of equal importance, you'll also learn what goes on inside my head, what I thought about before a game, in the on-deck circle, in the batter's box, and after every pitch. In many ways my philosophies are unique, but they are also well-grounded. In my 40 years around the major leagues, I've watched thousands of great and not-so-great hitters. I've seen what works and what doesn't, and I've sought to understand the fundamentals of success and failure. I've spent thousands of hours experimenting, watching videotape, and refining my own hitting techniques. In the end, I've developed a few basic beliefs and these 10 important keys to good hitting. (see next page)

10 Keys to Good Hitting

1. **Do not fear the baseball.** The greatest asset any hitter can have is to be fearless at the plate. You can't be afraid of being hit by the ball and be a good hitter.

2. **Stay within yourself.** Know who you are as a hitter, your strengths and weaknesses, and play within your abilities.

3. **Use your hands.** Become an "aggressive hands" hitter. This allows you to wait longer on the pitch and react to changes in pitch direction, both horizontally and vertically, in the strike zone.

4. **Be confident at the plate.** Know what you want to do when you get up to home plate. Combine purposes and discipline. Control the confrontation; that is, do what you want to do, not what the pitcher wants you to do.

5. **Stay flexible.** You can't be static in the batter's box. You must be able to keep your stance and outlook flexible enough to react to different pitches and situations

6. **Practice makes perfect.** Work hard to hone your skills, to fine-tune fundamentals. Be willing to pay the price of success, to put in the time necessary to compete against those athletes who pride themselves on a strong work ethic.

7. **Hit the ball where it's pitched.** Learn to utilize the entire field, foul line to foul line. Learn to hit the ball pitched down the middle *through* the middle, to pull the inside pitch, to slap the outside pitch the other way.

8. **Be aggressive.** Swing to make solid contact, to hit through the baseball, remembering not to become so aggressive you begin swinging at bad pitches and start pulling off the ball.

9. **Develop a one-component swing.** Strive to swing in one fluid motion, with all of your body parts functioning together. Avoid the step-turn-swing approach to hitting.

10. **Stay in shape.** Work year-round to put—and keep—your body in shape, to draw the most out of your physical abilities.

And now it's time for the lessons to begin. I've got all of the tools of learning laid out before me, so what do you say we turn you into a .300 hitter for life?

You can't be afraid of being hit by the ball and be a good hitter. A player who "bails out" sacrifices plate coverage and power. Don't allow your fear to play a role at the plate. Once you don't fear the ball, pitchers will start to fear you.

Fear

A lot of ballplayers are afraid to talk about fear, but it plays a pivotal role in the game, particularly the physical worry of being hit—and perhaps seriously injured—by a pitch. I was never afraid of getting hit, and that's one edge I had over some other players. Every ballplayer has a general concern about his physical safety—you have to. The sheer speed of some pitchers demands it. But the ones who carry the fear too far, who worry beyond reason, are the ones who get hurt the most. The reason? Simple. They freeze. They don't react. In anticipating a certain pitch, they leave themselves open—thinking curveball and getting a fastball—and when that happens they can't react as quickly, and they take a shot on the shoulder or leg . . . or worse.

To overcome this fear, have a friend throw some tennis balls or rubber balls at you from close range, 10 or 15 feet or so. Remember to react by swinging your back out *toward* the pitcher, thus protecting your face and head. After getting plunked a couple

Overcome your fear of being hit by the ball by having a parent or a friend softly throw a tennis ball at you from close range and then gradually move a little further away. This drill will help you understand that the ball really doesn't hurt.

of times with a rubber ball, you'll realize it's going to sting for a second or two, but what the heck, it's part of the game. That's the way former Houston Astros all-star Craig Biggio looked at it. A member of the 3,000-hit club, he was hit by more pitches than any other player in major league history—285 to be exact. He just said the heck with it, jogged down to first base, and forgot about it. You must learn to do the same.

Hitting Within Yourself

What kind of hitter are you now? What kind of hitter do you want to be? Does your swing need a complete overhaul or just a little fine-tuning? These are very important questions, one of the reasons "Stay within yourself" is No. 2 in the keys to good hitting. Yet at the same time, these simple questions beg other questions: Are you built for the long ball and, if so, do you connect or strike out a lot? Did you hit a lot of home runs in Little League or high school, but can't seem to connect now? Are you fast, but can't seem to hit the ball on the ground to take advantage of your speed? Are you always popping the ball up or pulling the ball into easy outs at short or second?

Before reading any further, sit down and ask yourself these questions. Think of who you are as a hitter and what type of hitter you'd like to be. Are they compatible? Can they ever be? Do you have the body of a Babe Ruth, but play the game of a Dustin Pedroia? If you can't figure out your problems, consult your

One key to becoming a good hitter is to stay within your own natural abilities. Each player has different strengths and weaknesses. The bigger boy in this picture is much more likely to be a power hitter than the smaller boy. Learn who you are as a hitter, stay disciplined, and you'll like the results.

parents or your coach. Are you trying to be the type of hitter you just aren't built to be? Analyze yourself; then go about deciding how you would like to change.

Some words of caution: You may not have to alter much at all; maybe what you need is to shift your weight around a bit or get a little more or less aggressive at the plate. But if you do have to change, ask yourself whether you are capable, *mentally*, of making these adjustments. Ego is a tough competitor. If you're too stubborn to admit you can't be the next King Kong of baseball, if you feel you *have* to pull every pitch, well, you may be wasting your time with this book. If you can't adjust when adjustment is necessary, that's fine. Just be prepared to start buying your tickets to baseball games.

Let me give you an example of being too stubborn for your own good. You're a fine young hitter with one problem: you can't hit the low fastball. Sure enough, soon enough, you strike out on just that pitch, then walk back to the bench muttering to yourself. The next time up, you adjust, which is good, but you make the wrong adjustment. Instead of working on hitting low fastballs in practice, you crouch down, attempting to cover the pitch. It doesn't work. A good catcher immediately calls for a high fastball. You swing and miss. So you straighten up. Then you get a low fastball. Now you're dumbfounded. You don't know what to think or how to stand. Instead of working on your weaknesses—taking batting practice with pitches thrown deliberately down low—you keep shifting around in the box and stay completely confused.

The answer to this problem can be summarized in two words: clear goals. Hall of Famer George Brett of the Kansas City Royals had clear goals. He knew what he could and could not do at the plate. Ichiro is the same way. So are the Twins' Joe Mauer and Texas' Michael Young. They don't pretend to be hitters they're not. They all accent the positive, they all make consistent contact, and they've all won batting titles. On the other side of the coin, there are many players consistently mired in the low .200s because they continually kid themselves; they try to be something they're not.

The rise of Justin Morneau really illustrates this point. In his first three seasons with the Minnesota Twins, beginning in 2003, he hit .226, .271, and .239 before jumping all the way up to .321 in 2006, when he became the American League MVP after also driving in 130 runs and hitting 34 homers. He improved because he put in the hard work and matured as a hitter. Instead of trying to pull the ball and hit home runs every time, he worked and learned to use both sides of the field. And he ended up hitting more home runs in the process, too.

Of course, Justin should have played to his strengths, to his abilities as a contact hitter, right away. But it takes time to discover who you are as a hitter and to develop a willingness to change. I'm not saying Justin shouldn't try occasionally to go deep, but one has to weigh his role on the ball club carefully. Players like Ryan Howard and Mark Reynolds, for example, know they're paid to hit the ball out of the park and not, in general, to hit .290. That's for other players, like their teammates hitting ahead of them in the order. So unless you're a young Miguel Cabrera, don't try to be someone you're not. Cabrera is, of course, another matter; he can help his team, the Detroit Tigers, by hitting 30 or more home runs a year, but he can do even more—as he did in 2010, hitting .328, with 38 homers and 126 RBI—by staying within himself, not trying for home runs. In Cabrera and in others with such a powerful stroke, like Ryan Braun of the Milwaukee Brewers (.320, 32 homers, and 114 RBI in 2009), home runs are simply the frequent result of making such strong, consistent contact with the pitch.

Confidence

It's true that confidence is a by-product of success, but if you're in the proper frame of mind when you walk up to the plate, no matter how well or poorly you've been playing, it's going to have a positive effect on your performance. Throughout my life, from childhood through my career in the major leagues, I always believed I was going to get a hit. *Every* time up. It never made any difference to me who was pitching. I wanted that pitcher to *feel* the confidence I had at the plate; I wanted every pitcher to know that I was the best there was and that when I stepped into the batter's box, he had his hands full.

I was also very greedy when it came to getting hits. I saw too many players get two hits in their first two at bats and mentally take the rest of the game off. "My day is made," they'd say. Not me. When I got two hits, I wanted three, then four, then five. Conversely, when I made an out, I made an out. I tipped my hat to the pitcher, made a mental note of why I failed, and forgot about it. But be assured that pitcher knew I was going to be an even tougher out the next time up.

Baseball is a mental game. There's no way around it. Most ballplayers who fail in the major leagues (and even at lower levels) do so because of weak minds, not weak bodies. Every time you step up to the plate the scene is set: pitcher versus hitter. Somebody is going to win. What you have to learn to guard against is getting too high or too low on any given day, avoiding the peaks and valleys and trying to stay on an even keel. If you're 5 for 5 today and 0

Every time you step up to the plate the scene is set: pitcher versus hitter. Somebody is going to win.

Always be confident at the plate. Baseball is a mental game. Know what you want to do when you get up to bat and keep a positive frame of mind by telling yourself you will get a hit every time. The key to your success as a hitter starts with the way you carry yourself.

for 5 tomorrow, you have to remember to take each ensuing at bat individually and not get too complacent or cocky about yourself.

The fear of failure is both the cause and the effect of prolonged slumps. If you don't believe you can hit, you won't hit. It's that simple. Also, if you go into a slump—as all of us do at one time or another—if you lose your confidence, pulling out of the slump will be twice as tough. Both of these psychological problems are much more common in the major leagues than one might believe, because baseball players, like most athletes, for all their bragging and macho image, have very gentle psyches. Another treatable form of fear might be called the "overmatched syndrome." It surfaces most often when my teammates say things like, "No use hitting against him tonight," or "We might as well just give him the game." You can't allow yourself to have that attitude, because if it's so-and-so one night, it will be somebody else the next and someone else after that. Pretty soon you've got a built-in bag of excuses for incorrect hitting. Take your cuts, no matter who's throwing or what he's throwing.

Practice makes perfect. You can't become the best without putting in the time. A few extra minutes of focus and discipline at games and practices can really pay off. The best athletes always tend to be the first ones on the field and the last ones to leave.

Another problem you'll find is that when you do begin to hit well, even in Little League, you become a marked man or woman. Coaches will pitch around you. They'll try to intimidate you, do anything—legal or illegal—to get you off your game. Plus, as you get older and the scouting and managing improve, your swing will be filmed, studied, and broken down like a piece of machinery, with everyone looking for the weak links. It's only a matter of time before someone will realize you don't like, say, a sharp-breaking inside curve, or you will chase a fastball up and out of the strike zone. You just have to realize there are days when you're going to make outs; after all, if you hit .300, you are still failing 7 out of 10 times. But you can't stop fixing those weak links, and soon enough they aren't so weak anymore. The only way to do that is with practice. Honest-to-goodness, grimy, T-shirt-soaked-in-sweat practice.

Perfect Practice Makes Perfect

For some guys, batting practice before a game or on an off-day is just an excuse to goof around, to play home-run derby. Personally, I try to hit the ball into the seats only when we're down by a run late in the game and we need runs in a hurry. On the whole, I dislike the long-ball attitude because of what I've seen it do to ballplayers. They get into a game situation where they must move a runner over, hit to the right side or uppercut a pitch to get a sacrifice fly, and they can't do it. They don't know how to do it. They haven't practiced it.

No matter how I'm hitting, I always take extra batting practice. It doesn't have to be a long, drawn-out affair, maybe 7 to 10 minutes extra on game day and 15 minutes at other times. But it helps, especially if you use the time wisely. Some days I'll work on a particular pitch I got a hit off the day before but, for some reason, felt funny executing. Maybe I was fooled and fought the ball off; maybe I was a little behind the pitch. Whatever, I'll ask my coaches to keep the ball in that spot during my workout so I can hit the pitch hard and correctly.

Train hard and maintain an overall healthy lifestyle. You can draw the most out of your physical abilities by staying in shape. This will carry into all aspects of the game and put you one step ahead of everyone else.

Ted Williams, the last of the .400 hitters, had similar theories about extra hitting. He couldn't get enough. Pete Rose was from the same school, as was Tony Gwynn. That's probably the biggest reason Tony was considered one of the best hitters of the 1980s and 1990s. It was no accident that when his manager, Dick Williams, was asked who would show up to hit at an optional practice during the 1984 World Series, he said, "If only one player showed up, it would be Tony Gwynn."

One final, often overlooked note on batting practice: I've always believed this is a time primarily for working on things you don't do well, leaving a little time to smooth over your strong points. Most players coming out of college today don't work on their weaknesses, a product of their success at lower levels where they were good enough to get by, and even dominate, without worrying about those weaknesses. But in the major leagues, and even in the minors, it's different. Weaknesses are quickly found and continually exploited until the player either adjusts or is replaced. Don't just go through the motions. Don't confuse activity with achievement. As legendary UCLA basketball coach John Wooden was fond of saying, "Practice doesn't make perfect, perfect practice makes perfect."

> **When your concentration is good, your confidence as a hitter naturally improves.**

Purpose and Concentration

No matter what the count, the situation, the surroundings, I've always tried to concentrate, to have a purpose with *every* pitch I've hit. I know sometimes it's impossible; your mind wanders. But it is important that you try to put yourself in an altered state whenever you step into the batter's box: a state where school, home, cars, friends, wives, or what you're having for dinner never enters; a state where your mind is focused on just a single object—the *baseball*. Just one white dot with 108 little stitches. You'll find that when your concentration is good, your confidence as a hitter naturally improves. It's also important to forget the past—whether you struck out the time before or if this pitcher reminds you of Nolan Ryan or you have three hits in three at bats. I can't remember ever being satisfied or complacent about anything I've done in the batter's box. Everything is done for a purpose, and that purpose is making the sweetest, most solid contact you possibly can.

I'm not a big fan of taking pitches. Why wait for the perfect pitch when, first, you may never see it, and second, you lose your aggressiveness waiting for it? If the pitch is *around* home plate and I'm confident I can *handle* it—that is, do something positive with the pitch—I'm swinging. I'm concerned by coaches, especially at lower levels of the game, who tell kids to "wait for a good

Be aggressive when hitting. Once you have committed to a good pitch, follow through without any hesitation. By swinging through the ball in one fluid motion, you will make solid contact and achieve positive results.

pitch" before they swing. To me, it's better to learn how to swing the bat and make contact than to wait all day for a pitch down the middle. A pitch may be out of the strike zone, but if you feel you can make solid contact, let 'er rip, especially if you're ahead in the count—2 and 0, 3 and 1—and geared for a certain pitch in your zone. Naturally, if you're behind in the count—say, 1 and 2—you have to be less selective, attacking anything that's close.

Over the years I've enjoyed watching certain hitters. One of my favorites was Frank Robinson because he was such a complete hitter. He always gave himself up for the team. He could hit with power and drive the ball deep into the opposite field. Pete Rose and George Brett are fine examples of hitters who played to—and beyond—their abilities. Rose made himself into a hitter, pure and simple, and George—well, George won batting titles in three different decades—so what does that tell you?

Chapter 1

Setting Up the Swing

Try a variety of different bat shapes and sizes. It may take some time and experimentation, but you'll ultimately find the bat that's right for you.

Choosing the Right Bat

I always had the greatest respect for my bats. I used a 34 1/2-inch-long, 32-ounce bat that was tooled from ash. The top was as wide as the rules allowed, which gave me a large contact surface. The handle was very narrow, about the width of a quarter—a combination of fat and thin that provided me the proper mix of power and quickness that I desired. But I'm not going to tell you which bat is right for you; there's no golden rule stating if you're this tall and weigh this much, X bat is right for you. It has as much to do with a person's strength, the type of hitter he is (not the type he wants to be), and, in some cases, what bat is available. I do, however, suggest experimenting with various lengths and handle sizes until you find the combination that you like and that works best for you.

But don't expect immediate results. It took me until 1970, my fourth year in the major leagues, to find my bat. Until then I was using heavy, 36-ounce jobs. One day in Lakeland, Florida, I was watching Al Kaline, the Tigers' Hall of Fame outfielder and a 3,000-hit man, take batting practice. When Al finished, I asked to see his bat. (It looked as though it bent when he whipped through his swing in the cage.) His bat was very thin and light—just 32 ounces—and very comfortable in my hands. I asked Kaline why he used this model. His answer was simple: it felt good. It was the same for Hank Aaron. He used a 32- or 33-ounce bat, and he could hit a baseball 500 feet. Current Major League all-star

This is a little trick I learned from Ted Williams. Early in the season, when I was stronger, I liked to use a longer, heavier bat. As the season went on I used a lighter, shorter model. But, I still wanted the bat to *seem* heavier and longer and vice versa. To make the bat seem longer, turn the label away from you. When you do this you see nothing but bat, and there is greater continuity. When you want the bat to seem shorter and lighter, turn the label toward you. The break in the continuity will create the illusion of a shorter bat. Yes, I know we're talking about an illusion, but take every advantage you can as a hitter.

Albert Pujols has used various sizes of bat, but he primarily goes with a 34- or 34 1/2-inch bat weighing 32 ounces. Neither felt he had to tote a tree trunk up to home plate, and over two vastly different eras they have hit more than 1,100 home runs between them—and counting. So don't get caught up in those mind games that people play, the ones with rules like, "The bigger the bat the better the bang." It's a myth.

Tony Gwynn is considered one of the greatest hitters of all time and certainly of his generation. He had a Hall of Fame career using the smallest bat in history at 31 inches. Whether it was in the 1970s, 1980s, 1990s, or the new millennium, great hitters have proved that you don't need a big bat to be a big-time hitter—you need the right bat for you.

Bear in mind that the comfortable feel of a bat is the key. For example, I did change bats on occasion, replacing my regular bat late in the season with a shorter, lighter model. By that point in the season my arms were tired and I didn't want to lose any quickness, so I sacrificed some weight. Also remember that finding good balance in a bat is important.

Once you've selected a bat, treat it with respect. I cleaned all my bats of excess dirt and pine tar religiously so they didn't pick up extra weight. Plus, I like the look of a clean bat and a clean, fresh uniform. It says a lot about your sense of pride. And I didn't like teammates or strangers picking up or swinging my bats. My feeling was that they were my property, and I didn't want "unauthorized personnel" handling them. On a trip to New York, shortly after I got my three thousandth hit, six of my bats "disappeared" from the locker room at Yankee Stadium. I can't tell you how upsetting that was. I started to understand why Pete Rose carried his own bats.

Finally, when it comes to selecting "good wood," I'll let you in on a couple of trade secrets. Look for bats on which the streaks of grain are farthest apart; it's a sign of solid stock. Also, check for a bat with knots on the surface; they're the hardest part of any wood. You can also harden a bat by "boning" it, rubbing the bat along the grain with a hard butcher's bone or another baseball bat. This compresses the wood, making it doubly solid on the surface. Another trick of mine, one unfortunately not available to too many players below the major league level, is to keep your bats next to a sauna. The dry heat from the sauna bakes out the bad or weak spots in the wood and reduces splintering. In the offseason I kept my bats in a box filled with sawdust and placed them in a warm place in my house. The sawdust acts as a buffer between the bats and the environment, absorbing any moisture before it can seep into the wood.

One final thought: aluminum bats have taken over on every level of baseball outside the professional ranks for one reason: it's much more economical to buy bats that last all season than

A basic diagram showing the essential parts of a baseball bat. *Shutterstock*

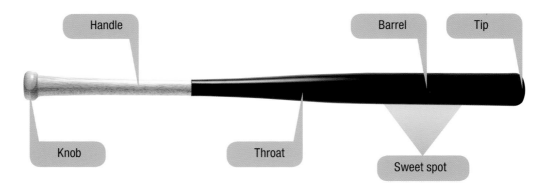

When you select your bats, remember that traditional wisdom says the wider apart the streaks of grain, the more solid the stock. The grain on this gamer is pretty good. Good wood/bad wood, however, is often overrated. Make solid contact on the sweet spot of any good bat and you will be rewarded.

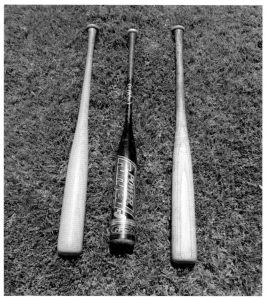

Aluminum bats are the worst thing to happen to developing hitters, as they create a false sense of accomplishment and ability. Bad habits are rewarded when sure outs with a wooden bat are rewarded with aluminum base hits. If you want to become the best hitter you can be, use your aluminum bat in games, but practice with a wooden bat. Recent legislation to "dial down" aluminum bats and make them respond more like wood is a good thing.

bats that break. But aluminum bats also give you a false sense of accomplishment at the plate. Too many players pick up bad habits because they get base hits off those inside pitches that would have been sure outs with a wooden bat. It's something scouts take into consideration these days when charting a prospect. And I think it's to your advantage, if you have the desire and potential to be a major league player, to use a wooden bat—if not in your games, at least in batting practice. A wooden bat will show your true talents. So, it's good to see that in certain high schools they're ushering in the use of wood bats for safety reasons. They're safer for your well-being and your future as a hitter.

Find a bat you can swing—not one that swings you.

The Grip

Ty Cobb choked up on the bat and used a split grip, with a 1-inch gap between the bottom and top hands. His average over 24 major league seasons? Only .367. Mickey Mantle, meanwhile, hit 536 home runs for the New York Yankees in 18 big-league seasons. His grip? The bottom hand so far down the handle of the bat that his pinky finger curled around the bottom of the knob.

The moral to this is that there are no absolutes in gripping a baseball bat. In general, common sense and comfort are the keys to the proper grip. You want to keep things simple, to get the job done without making too big a mess, and there are all sorts of ways to go about it. Most major-leaguers today lean toward nothing more than "what's comfortable." That often means holding the bat in an area of the hands where the palm ends and the fingers begin, the alignment no more complex than lining up your knuckles. By that I mean that the knuckles on the first joint of each hand should be in a line. There is nothing wrong with this grip except that it's the only grip many coaches teach.

If aligning the knuckles is not comfortable, experiment and find a grip that is, and that's not hard to do. Just pick up your bat and let your fingers do the talking. Be as natural as possible, not putting the bat too far forward in your fingers or too far back in your palms. Imagine playing a trumpet or saxophone. Feel the wood; don't grip the bat too tightly. Tension is your enemy, and in one easy lesson I can show you why.

Make a fist with either hand. Look at the inside of your wrist, at the tendons. See the strain? Feel the tightness? Of course you do. Now pull your fingers into a fist but don't hold so tightly. See the difference when you look at your wrist? That extra tension inhibits your ability to generate bat speed because the wrists and forearms—sources of hand speed and power—are tied into knots.

My preference is to grip the bat very lightly with my bottom hand. My bottom hand (since I hit from the left side, my right hand) exerts very little pressure, acting almost like a rudder to keep my swing on course. My hands stay loose as they come back to launch position, tightening as I make my approach to the ball. The top hand should *never* clamp down hard on the bat; rather, it should maintain a firm grip. This makes you (a) a more relaxed hitter, and (b) a more flexible hitter, capable of maneuvering the bat quickly and efficiently through the strike zone.

It is equally important to take care of your hands (I've made a great living with mine). Treat them carefully, lovingly. I never went around smashing my hands into water coolers; I don't attack

Common sense and comfort are the keys to a proper grip. Keep things simple and you'll find a grip that works for you.

Find a grip that is comfortable for you. I prefer the bat loosely held toward my fingers (top left). Other players like the bat in either the front part (top right) or the back part (bottom) of their palms. There is no right way or wrong way. Experiment with the bat and find out what feels right for you.

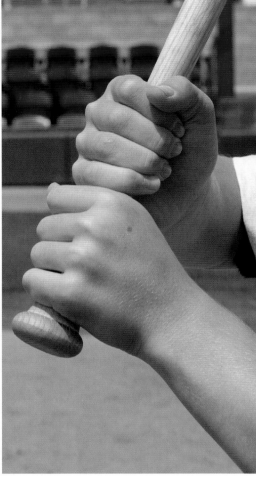

Compare the two photos. Notice how the knuckles line up in one of the photos and they do not line up in the other. The knuckles in my grip did not line up. Many coaches teach lining up the knuckles, but again, as with the grip, the only right way is what works for you.

lockers or walls. Those are fights you cannot win. On the bat, I hold them loosely, free of tension, believing that if you're going to squeeze the bat upon contact anyway, why force the issue? Keeping my hands loose allows me to maneuver the bat better, decreases upper-body tension, and it allows me to attack certain pitches that, if my hands were wrapped tightly around the lumber, I'd never get to in time.

Once you're settled on a grip, it's time to figure out where you want to place your hands on the bat. For certain hitters, I advocate choking up a bit, moving your hands up off the bottom. This not only quickens and shortens the stroke but also increases your maneuverability.

Batting Gloves

Batting gloves have been a part of the game for roughly 35 years now, and I think they've been an improvement. Certainly, using a glove during batting practice cuts down on the sting after a long session and reduces blisters and calluses on the hands. I'm also in favor of wearing them in the field, as they add a little extra padding.

Richard Paul Kran/Shutterstock.com

If you're a head-first slider, it can also be beneficial to use batting gloves on the base paths. Holding a glove in each hand on the bases forces you to form a fist, preventing you from extending your fingers when sliding headfirst into a base and thereby reducing the risk of injury. Then again, as has become a hot topic, sliding feet-first will always cut down on injury. For me personally, I always tried to slide with my feet hitting the bag first because I wanted to protect my hands. After all, it was my hands that I made a living with, just like every other successful hitter.

The only caution with batting gloves, as with any equipment, is not to get too emotionally tied to them. If you happen to lose them or leave them at home, you can't let it affect your play.

Batting gloves, like any piece of equipment, can also become subject to superstition. Don't let them become an excuse for an out or compromise your at bat. Equipment's important, sure. But whether it's a special pair of batting gloves or how many times you strap and unstrap your gloves between each pitch, it should never become a distraction or an excuse.

Don't squeeze the grip until the bat turns to sawdust. Loose hands are the source of hand speed, and the speed of the bat through the hitting zone is a key to good hitting. These two angles show a nice, soft grip on the bat. The bottom hand is relaxed and exerts very little pressure on the bat. The top hand is doing little more than cradling the bat. Neither hand will tighten its grip until just prior to contact.

Choking Up on the Bat

One of the remnants of baseball's past that hasn't survived too well in the last 30 years is the style of "choking up"—moving the hands up—on the bat. Though today's players may be better athletes, the old-timers were on to something when they decided to choke up.

Baseball history was written by men like Cobb and Wee Willie "Hit-'em-where-they-ain't" Keeler, choke-up artists who lived by one rule: to get a hit, you first had to hit the ball. In recent years, only Rose and Barry Bonds come to mind as players who consistently moved their hands more than an inch or two off the bottom of the bat.

With rare exception, a hitter who chokes up on the bat has to accept the fact that he is not a home-run hitter. Pete once said that he wanted to be the first singles hitter to drive a Cadillac. He ended up driving a Rolls-Royce, so you'd have to say that hitting singles was very good to him. With 3,215 singles to his credit, Pete is baseball's all-time leader in that category. [Editor's note: Carew is seventh, with 2,404.]

Choking up on the bat gives you more good wood to work with. It also makes the bat shorter, and though this limits your

Choking up can help a hitter make better contact, something I am all in favor of. Not only does choking up give a hitter better bat control, but for some reason a hitter seems to concentrate more when choking up.

reach somewhat, it makes you concentrate harder to lay off marginal pitches that you can't drive. It's interesting to see how that extra concentration makes better hitters out of players who do shorten up on the bat after they have two strikes. If they hit all the time as they did with two strikes, they'd probably hit 20 points higher.

How much should you choke up? Like most other things in hitting, there is no definitive answer. Play with the bat and find an area that feels comfortable for you. You're obviously not going to choke up to the label, but 1 or 2 inches should begin to get you into the comfort zone. And don't worry about what the other kids will say. I'd rather choke up and play all the time than swing from the end of the bat and sit on the bench. Just in case you're wondering, I didn't choke up, but that was only because I liked to have the extra bat length. I felt confident and comfortable knowing what pitches I could hit and that I would make good, consistent contact without choking up.

Barry Bonds

Exceptional Choke-Up Artist

The obvious exception to the notion that a hitter who chokes up on the bat can't hit for power is Barry Bonds. Barry could hit for power to every part of the field and never felt he sacrificed any plate coverage by choking up. The fact that he stood fearlessly close to the plate—almost on top of it—probably helped compensate for the few inches of reach he lost by choking up. Barry had a short, precise swing that made the most of his exceptional hands. In his 22-year career in the big leagues, choking up on the bat allowed him to be a sensational hitter for both average and power—with a .298 lifetime batting average and, of course, 762 home runs.

Barry Bonds had great success choking up on the bat, hitting for both average and power throughout his record-filled career. *AP Photo*

Chapter 2 The Stance

Your stance is the foundation of your swing. Take your time.

Think of a marvelous meal set on a beautiful, colored tablecloth made of fine linen and served in shining silver and sparkling crystal. Then imagine rushing through this meal at breakneck speed, not enjoying either the food or the setting.

I can't believe how many ballplayers fire through their at bats at the same speed. Instead of taking their time, setting up in the box, enjoying the meal, they rush right through an at bat as if they were eating in a fast-food restaurant. Your stance is the foundation of your swing. Take your time. Don't treat it lightly. You must not feel silly, particularly in the early stages of a stance adjustment, in taking a few extra seconds in the batter's box. You should always run down a little mental list: Are the feet set? Can you cover the plate with your bat? These are all things you work on in practice so that, come game time, they are automatic.

Over the years much has been said and written about my style of hitting, about the different positions I assumed in the box, how I moved around from at bat to at bat, from pitch to pitch. It's certainly true that, on occasion, I adjusted my stance from pitcher to pitcher, even pitch to pitch, but I would like to lay to rest one of the biggest misconceptions about my stance: *I did not move around in the batter's box.* My back foot didn't move for the last 15 years of my career. Only my front foot moved, shifting open or closed in relation to the situation at hand.

Because of this misconception, some said I was the only person who could hit "on the move." Nonsense. If a young hitter wanted

I suggest that hitters set up deep in the batter's box to get a longer look at the ball and close to home plate to get maximum plate coverage. Don't worry about being jammed; that's determined by the position of your front foot. I also don't buy the theory that if you get forward in the box you can hit the curve before it breaks. When you get forward in the box the pitcher will see it and adjust accordingly, throwing his pitch 2 feet shorter so the break is the same.

to work at it and find the comfort I've found, using what I call the flexible stance, fine. Stronger players in general don't make big adjustments in their stances—the great Reggie Jackson's swing was open a bit, swinging in from his heels—but to be a consistent hitter, I believe you need to be able to adjust, to adapt your game to the pitcher. The changes are not major; normally I made minor mechanical adjustments, not to the *kind* of pitch but to the location of it. This gave me a much better chance of seeing the baseball. But you just can't use any stance for a day, a week, or two weeks and expect big results. I've worked with guys who have tried one stance, found it comfortable, then had a bad day or two. The first change they make is right back to their old way of hitting, and in their haste and insecurity they never really give themselves a chance to become comfortable—and confident—with this crucial part of the hitting process.

The Carew Flex-Stance

As with any good, solid stance, the flex-stance begins with your feet. They should generally be about shoulder width apart, facilitating an easy weight transfer from the back foot to the front as the ball approaches what I call the contact zone. For me, the contact zone means the area just off the front foot, about a foot in front of the plate. Just how far the contact zone extends out in front of home plate depends on the location of the pitch. But the general rule of thumb is this: the location of the pitch from outside to inside is in direct proportion to how far out front you want to make contact. In other words, if the pitch is outside, wait a split second longer before swinging. If it's down the middle, attack a bit earlier, and even earlier for an inside pitch.

The contact zone is that area, just off your front foot and in front of home plate, where the bat meets the ball. To keep the ball in play, you must contact the ball *in front of* home plate. The further in front of home plate your bat is upon contact, the more you will pull the ball. The closer you are to the front of home plate upon contact, the more you will hit to the opposite field.

The stance is the foundation of your swing. It is as unique as you are. You need to be comfortable, you need to be flexible, you need to be balanced, and as discussed earlier, you need to be able to cover the plate. Take your time and experiment until you find the exact stance that's right for you.

The reasons are many: First, the deeper a ball gets into the strike zone, the harder it is to hit it fair. Second, as mentioned, the wickedest movement on fastballs and curves often comes in the last 2 to 3 feet before they reach the plate. Finally, your hands and hips come into play in front of the plate. If you're slow, if the ball gets "in" on you, your body tightens, you lose arm extension, and you can't get the fat part of the bat on the ball. In short, your license to drive the ball has been taken away. So, to keep the ball in play, to move it around the diamond, to hit the best part of a pitch, contact the ball *out in front of the plate*.

Also, much has been written about the need for a "balanced" stance, as opposed to leaning too far forward on your front foot or too far backward on your rear foot. It is important to start from a centered, balanced position. My first move was back, then my stride took me back to a centered position where I hit.

Balance is the most important key to good hitting.

Where to Stand

Okay, we've decided how we're going to distribute our weight. Now, where do you place the back foot? For this, there are as many opinions as there are fans in the stands. Some people prefer to stand deep in the box, others want to remain even with the plate, and still others prefer to have their front foot beyond the front edge of home plate. Once that decision has been made, you must decide how close to the plate you want to be. Are you better off standing on top of the plate? A few inches or a few feet away?

Whatever the final decision, remember: in every one of these situations you're giving up something to get something. Stand close to the plate and you'll certainly get coverage on the outside corner, but, inevitably, you'll find yourself in a position to be worked to death inside. And what about having that front foot so far forward as to be beyond the plate? Great for hitting the curve before it breaks, but trouble when a guy has a 90-mile-per-hour fastball that he can cut any way he wants. My advice is this: Move your back leg along the back line, near the *inside* chalk mark of the box. This places you deep in the box and fairly close to home plate, giving you time to wait on the pitch. With a flexible *front* leg, you have the ability to adjust, to open or close the stance, depending on the pitcher and even, at times, the pitch.

I know, I know. A lot of you out there don't like that advice. You think hitting that far back in the box or that close to the plate limits your ability to hit the curveball. But in my experience, pitchers with good curves can break it off either in front or in back of the box. (They just shorten or lengthen their delivery.) Thus, the front-of-the-box argument is a weak one. For me, staying back bought me time to see the type and direction of the pitch. By increasing my reaction time, it gave me a chance to adjust to surprises.

Now, with this back leg planted, we can get into the main distinctions of the flex-stance. The key to this stance is the front foot. My front-foot setup dictated everything I did at the plate. I treat my back foot as a hinge and my front foot as a gate to swing open and closed, depending on who's pitching and what he throws.

Plate coverage is critical to good hitting. You must make sure your bat comfortably reaches the outside black of home plate and a little beyond. When you step into the batter's box, develop a routine of taking your bat and touching just beyond the outside corner of home plate, closest to the pitcher, and then the outside corner of home plate, closest to the catcher. If you can cover this portion of the plate in your setup you will be able to cover any strike after you've taken your stride toward the pitch.

My standard stance from the flex position is medium open, my front leg anywhere from 8 to 12 inches from the inside chalk line. This allows me to turn my head so that both eyes face the pitcher, making for good sightlines on most of the pitches thrown. I used this stance 80 percent of the time.

The front foot, meanwhile, is not lying flat on the ground like those of most players. Rather, the heel is elevated about 2 inches, a change I made early in my career because I didn't feel I was getting enough mobility in my hips and legs, and I wanted to be able to "turn" on a pitch more quickly. With the heel up, the pivot off that front toe is much faster because you don't have to raise your foot to turn. Also, when you stride, you don't come down heavily on that front foot, but instead land softly on the toes, which allows you to increase leverage and open up more quickly on inside pitches. The front leg is straight but somewhat loose, just firm enough to support the hip rotation but not rigid. If you commit that leg, locking it, flexibility is lost, and you can't adjust to the ball's inside or outside movement. The only time that the leg should lock is *after* contact is made and the hands are released. The two other key positions of the flex-stance are as follows:

Open. Front foot 12 to 18 inches off the inside chalk. Used in situations where the pitcher regularly throws inside or when facing a sidearm curveball pitcher who throws from your side of the plate.

I liked to hit out of an open stance. I felt I could see the ball a little better, and being open helped me clear my hips faster on an inside pitch. Some people mistakenly believe that hitting from an open stance makes it harder to hit an outside pitch. Nothing can be further than the truth, because whether you choose an open stance or a closed stance, your first step is always *toward the pitcher.*

Here is an exaggerated closed stance. I am more concerned about this young hitter being too far up in the box than I am about his closed stance. As with the open stance, as long as your stride is toward the pitch and you hit the ball out in front of the plate, you will be successful.

Closed. This stance moves you closer to the plate. Front foot closer to the chalk line, no longer parallel to the back foot. Used principally against pitchers who consistently paint the outside corners or have a fastball or slider that runs away from the hitter.

Important: Because your front foot is mobile, and because it is natural to fear the baseball, the tendency is to "pull out," to take your first step away from home plate regardless of whether your stance is open or closed. This is wrong. Don't give in to the temptation. The first step should *always* be right back up the middle, right back at the pitcher. This discourages the disastrous tendency, particularly in the medium and open stances, to pull off a pitch on the inner half of the plate, which in turn takes your head and shoulders out, away from the ball.

When to Be Flexible

You can use all three stances in the same at bat, but the real key is knowing when to make your move. Baseball is not a computer sport. You don't punch up one key and always get the same answer. It's a subtle science with a pitcher mixing three, maybe four excellent pitches he can spot wherever he wants, working in concert with a catcher whose job it is to think one step ahead of the hitter, to keep the batter off balance and powerless. As I said before, I was never a guess hitter; rather, I was more of a situational hitter, a "tendency" hitter, someone who was prepared with a working knowledge of the pitcher I was facing *before* I stepped up to the plate. I studied my opponents and knew, in advance, *what* they liked to throw, *where* they liked to throw it, and *when* they liked to throw it. In major league baseball, it's obviously easier to make these judgments, to pick up patterns. We know who we'll be facing on a day-to-day basis, and our teams all have scouting departments to help prepare us on just what to expect from our opponents. And if they don't know, chances are

Baseball is not a computer sport, it's a subtle science.

someone in the dugout has played with or against this new face somewhere along the line in college or the pros. So we can pick up his pattern fairly quickly, if he hasn't changed.

But that's not to say you can't do a little scouting of your own. You have to if this flex-stance is going to work. Look to see how a pitcher warms up before the game and between innings. Watch how they pitch to the hitters ahead of you in the lineup. Do they try to set them up, or do they go with the hard stuff? Are they afraid to pitch inside? Do they like to throw a sinker or curveball when they're ahead in the count? When do you see the fastball? Also, talk to your teammates hitting ahead of you in the lineup and check out the movement of pitches thrown to them. By doing this, you'll walk into the batter's box prepared, knowing what stance to use. You'll be hitting from a position of strength, not weakness.

Usually, however, no matter who's pitching, I liked to start out with my medium-open stance, adjusting as I saw fit. In some situations that may be the second pitch, if the first pitch happened

I used to experiment with my swing all the time. When I came up as a rookie I was more upright. I found that I wasn't as flexible as I wanted to be, so early on I made my first major adjustment to flatten my bat. Later on, I crouched even more to force fastball pitchers like Nolan Ryan to bring the ball down to me. That adjustment worked, and from that point on I tinkered with my stance, sometimes even from pitch to pitch. However, I *never* moved in the batter's box. My back foot was in the same spot in the batter's box on my 9,315th major league at bat as it was on my first in 1967.
Ron Vesely/MLB Photos/Getty Images

to be called a strike and I knew, from experience, that when this pitcher was ahead early in the count he tended to throw the curveball inside. So I'd move that front gate, that foot, open a bit, allowing myself a little extra room inside to turn on the pitch. But, again, I wasn't guessing curveball, just the tendency of this pitcher to come inside. Even with the slightly more open stance, because I was always stepping straight toward the mound, I figured I should be able to handle any pitch.

Mind Games

Can you dictate from the setup position what kind of pitch you want thrown? Absolutely. I feel if he's thinking, any hitter can set up a pitcher. Why not? They do it to us all the time.

With this flex-stance it's possible to dictate pitches without sacrificing a swing or a turn at bat. On the occasions when I've wanted a pitch on the inside of the plate, I've leaned over with my hands and head and closed my front foot a couple of inches. When the pitcher and catcher see this, they invariably think "fastball inside." They think I'm afraid of not reaching the outside for the pitch. But as soon as the ball leaves the pitcher's hand and I see it's coming to the inside corner, I'm ready to open up that front leg and turn on the ball. Even if I don't pull it, I can still get good wood on the pitch and hit up the middle or to the opposite field.

Now, what happens when pitchers wise up to this maneuver and use some reverse psychology on you? What if he sees your adjustment, knows you're really looking for an inside pitch, and keeps the ball outside? Simple. You don't do a thing. Just swing away. That is the beauty of the flexible front foot. If you can learn to pick up the ball soon enough (something I'll discuss in the next chapter), you should be able to stay one step ahead of your enemy, because a pitcher can't change location once he's delivered a pitch. That's when you make your move.

You can learn to set the pitcher up with your stance at the plate.

You can also learn to set the pitcher up with your stance at the plate. Maybe you crouch a bit lower or stand up a bit straighter in your stance if the pitcher tends to aim for one particular level of the strike zone. You could be standing straight, but when he gets ready to pitch you might bend your knees a little. I did this spontaneously toward the end of my career, because it's something I experimented with for many years and I grew comfortable with it. But for you my suggestion would be to practice three or four different stances as the pitcher is about to deliver.

I know what you're thinking. There are a million different combinations of stances. How do you decide what stance is right in what situation? I limited myself to three or four basic stances that, given the starting pitcher and the relievers the opposing team had, I anticipated using that day. I also worked on hitting pitches in certain directions off certain stances. For example, from an upright stance, I'd force myself to hit on top of the ball. Or let's say a sinkerball pitcher is working, a pitcher who keeps the ball down around the knees. I would have a preset plan of what I wanted to do, which was to adjust my stance *down*, not move my front leg in or out. Because of the sinkerball, I'd crouch a little more at the plate to get down to the level so I could see the ball better and handle the pitch. The reason is simple. If the pitcher is throwing sinkers on the outside corner and I'm standing straight up, there's no way I can get good wood on that pitch. That's the problem with hitters who set up very straight. They don't have the flexibility in their legs to go down and get a pitch.

To me, every at bat was like a fine meal. Take your time. Enjoy the experience. *You* should dictate the at bat, not the pitcher. Don't let the pitcher rush you in and out of the batter's box. It's okay to ask for time-out. If it's good enough for Derek Jeter, it's good enough for you.

Former Yankees great Don Mattingly, who went on to manage the Dodgers, was one of the most flexible. He was able to make adjustments in his hitting approach not only during a ballgame but also during an at bat. Let me share a story with you about Mattingly from the 1985 season. Late in the season, both of our teams were involved, unsuccessfully as it turned out, in a heated pennant race. As so often happens, the Angels went out and purchased some late-season pitching help. In this case it was John Candelaria, a hard-throwing left-handed pitcher who had been a 20-game winner for the Pirates in the National League. Whenever you are seeing a pitcher for the first time, the pitcher has the advantage, and the game we were playing in was Candy's debut against the Yankees. To make things doubly difficult, Candelaria had a three-quarter-sidearm delivery, which is very intimidating to left-handed hitters.

During this particular game, in the middle innings, Mattingly came to the plate for a second time against Candy. I noticed he had altered his stance from the previous at bat. Naturally this interested me. He had closed his right shoulder substantially, and I couldn't wait to talk to him about it. Don walked during that at bat, so, as he stood on first, he and I talked about his strategy. He told me he had found that during his first at bat he had a tendency to want to release his upper body too soon against the left-handed sidearm offerings of Candelaria, so as he stepped in to face him a second time, he decided he would close his upper body—by that I mean he would show more of his back to the pitcher. This, he felt, would force him to keep his front shoulder in longer and would delay his mechanics—the movements of his swing—making him wait longer on the curveball and slider. Don practiced that adjustment and executed it at just the right time.

Good hitters spoil good pitches, disrupting a pitcher's concentration.

One of the most important points relative to the flex-stance is that you remain, as much as possible, on the same plane as the ball. By this I mean that you can't very easily swing up on a pitch that's down or, conversely, swing down on a pitch that's up in the strike zone. In general, if a pitch is right down the middle, belt-high, your swing should be perfectly flat. If the pitch is down at the knees or below, you shouldn't bend at the waist to hit it, but rather use your flexible legs to move your entire body in line to hit that pitch. And you can't be down in a crouch and bounce up to go after a high pitch. If you do, 9 times out of 10 you'll find yourself swinging and missing, taking a bad swing, or popping the ball up. You have to let your legs adjust to your body or learn to lay off a pitch that is not on your plane.

Obviously, the one time you can't afford to lay off is with two strikes and a borderline pitch that could be strike three. You have to

Need more proof that your stance is unique to you? Consider the great Stan Musial. You couldn't find two stances more different than Stan's and mine, yet we won 14 batting titles and had 6,683 total hits between the two of us. Despite our different stances, our hands were in the same position through the hitting zone, and that's the critical element in hitting. *Photo File/MLB Photos/Getty Images*

swing. But, in that case, with two strikes you wouldn't want to anticipate too much, crouching so low you couldn't swing and at least foul off a pitch at the top of the strike zone. Good hitters spoil good pitches. This can sometimes disrupt a pitcher's concentration because when he knows that you can spoil his best pitch in a crucial situation, he will really have his work cut out for him.

Some of the setup position is personal preference—that is, "what's comfortable"—but understand some basic dos and don'ts: Hold your bat too high and you'll find that as time goes on, as the pitching gets faster and more sophisticated, you'll be late getting the bat into the contact zone. Hold your hands too low and you'll have to move them up to get into hitting position. This wastes time, time you don't have, particularly against power pitchers. Hold your hands too close to the body and you'll find yourself "tied up," not being able to get the bat head into the contact zone. You're also inviting yourself to see a steady diet of inside fastballs that will crack more than their fair share of bats in two. Most ballplayers seem to find common ground with their hands back, about even with their back shoulder, top hand near the tip of their shoulder.

Chapter 3 Reading the Spin

Reading the spin takes concentration, observation, and the ability to master a few common rules.

Tennis players call it being "in the zone." In baseball it is often described in less cosmic but certainly no less meaningful terms. When we're "seeing the ball," the results are often out of this world: 4- and 5-hit games, 20-game hitting streaks, a home-run rampage. For some reason, when you're seeing the ball, it's bigger; you pick it up sooner; your reactions are quick and direct. Faster reading of spin tips off what kind of pitch is on the way, giving you an extra and valuable advantage over other hitters. And it's not that difficult. It takes concentration, observation, and the ability to master a few common rules.

Many ballplayers get into the habit of playing mind games with the pitcher and catcher. Of course, it's important to know what a guy has thrown, what he can throw; it alerts you to what's coming. And, sure, pitchers do throw in patterns—though, because of better coaching, not as much as they did 10 or 15 years ago. In the old days you wouldn't see a change-up or a breaking ball on 3–2 or 2–2. Now I see screwballs on 3–2, changes on 3–0 or 3–1, forkballs on 2–0. Of course, in Little League, junior high, and high school, the patterns are more predictable, though much depends on the pitcher himself. Does he want to get ahead of the hitter? Can he get his curve over for a strike? In high school, pitchers often don't have any idea of how they want to pitch. So it is best to anticipate their best pitch in a clutch situation. Why? It's a pitch they can control, and they don't want to get

Focus is important in every at bat. Know where to look. Don't be mesmerized by everything going on around you. Focus on that guy on the mound.

hurt with less than their best stuff. But beware: this isn't easy. If you're guessing the wrong pitch, you can't adjust. So, don't guess, at least not at the type of pitch. It's all right to look for location, but I, for one, always looked for one pitch: the fastball. I prepared myself mentally and physically for it on every delivery, for one basic reason: it moves at upward of 90 miles an hour, and reacting to it takes the ultimate in hand–eye coordination. Every other pitch is slower, be it a slider, curve, screwball, or change-up. If you're geared to hit a fastball, you can easily delay your mechanics to allow for a slower pitch. If, however, you're "sitting on"—guessing at, waiting for—a 70-plus-mile-an-hour curveball, there is no way you can accelerate your mechanics quickly enough to react to a faster pitch. So anticipate a fastball and allow your reactions, your patience, and your discipline to handle everything else.

Rule No. 1: Know Where to Look

Every pitcher has a release point, the point at which the ball leaves his hand, and it is the exact spot at which a hitter should begin to read the pitch. With a few exceptions, the most successful pitchers release all their pitches from the same spot. This is a mixed blessing, in that the hitter knows exactly where to look for every pitch, but then again, the pitcher is able to effectively camouflage his pitches. You will find pitchers, especially at lower levels, who tip their pitches by releasing different pitches from different points. The fastball is released over the top, above the ear; the curveball is also released above the ear, but from a higher arm slot. It's your job to learn the release point of each pitcher you face. If a pitcher

The release point is a constant, as is arm speed. Pitchers who consistently throw strikes always release their pitches from the same release point.

In order to reduce distractions when you're ready to hit, focus on the logo on the pitcher's hat. That never changes. No matter what herky-jerky mannerisms a pitcher may have, the logo on the hat is a constant, changing only from pitcher to pitcher.

is nice enough to tip his pitches, take note—just don't get lazy and resort to guessing.

It takes only half a dozen pitches or so to figure out where the fastball is released from and how, if at all, the release point may differ from those of his other pitches. Even if you're the lead-off hitter, by your second at bat you should pretty much have the pitcher pegged. And—just between you and me—keep an eye on your own pitchers. In most cases they will not be your teammates for life. You'll probably be opponents someday, whether it's in American Legion, high school, college, or the pros. It doesn't hurt to have some personal information on that pitcher filed away in your head for down the road.

Stay on the logo of the pitcher's hat until the pitcher makes his turn and breaks his hands. From there, go straight to his release point. Notice how short a distance it is from the logo on the hat to the release point. It's a simple movement of the eyes. The head stays still.

Rule No. 2: Know When to Look

Some players say the best way to pick up the baseball is to watch the entire motion from start to finish. Never take your eyes off the pitcher, they say. Not me. If you stare too long at the mound, you become mesmerized, so I never concentrated on the ball when it was in the pitcher's glove. Instead, while the pitcher was just standing on the rubber, I was preparing myself at the plate, relaxing my hands, working on my rhythm. I'd remain in that mode until the pitcher wound up, then I drew both my hands and front foot back, setting up my swing. When I focused on the pitcher, I locked onto the logo of his ball cap. Only *after* the hands break from the glove did I pick up the ball. From the cap, I went straight to the release point, where I again picked up the ball. Within 15 to 20 feet after the ball was released, I had computed the spin and knew whether a fastball or an off-speed pitch was on the way. Don't think for a second this is some simple equation. It's not. You have to *concentrate*. Often you find a pitcher who can make the ball dance, moving it up or down or in or out. Thus, it's important to know the characteristics of every pitch—how, for example, a slider moves about 10 miles an hour slower than a fastball, breaking about 3 feet from home plate. The more you know about a pitch, the quicker you can decide what to do with it and the longer you can wait. And—the key to all this—the longer you wait on a pitch, the better a hitter you'll be.

However tricky a pitcher's motion may be, it doesn't matter if you train your eyes to go from hat logo to release point. This pitcher's underhand motion is built for confusion, but his release point still tells us he's going to come under the ball.

This pitcher is about to release a fastball, and he's gripping the ball with the seams. Notice that his fingers are above the ball, which causes the fastball to appear to rise as it approaches the plate.

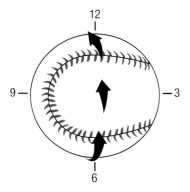

Fastball spin when thrown across the seams.

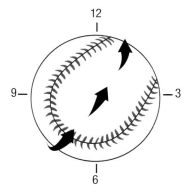

Fastball spin when thrown with the seams. The spin direction of a cut fastball is very similar.

Reading the Spin

The prospect of picking out rotation on a baseball traveling at a speed approaching 90 miles per hour, from a distance of some 55 feet, is enough to boggle the mind. And well it should. If that isn't tough enough, few ballplayers, particularly at the lower levels, know *what* to look for, even if they are looking. They don't know how a certain pitch rotates when thrown, say, across the seams, or how a curve or slider spins. Reading the spin is a delicate science. But once you begin to master it, the rewards are worth all the effort. You'll begin seeing the ball earlier and earlier, enabling you to program your mind faster, allowing you to wait longer before making a decision to swing. You'll also stop chasing pitches out of the strike zone. With all these possibilities in mind, let's discuss the specific spin on the most common pitches.

Fastball

The fastball comes in two varieties. One is thrown with the fingers gripping the ball across the seams, the other with the pitcher gripping the ball *with* the seams. Each pitch shares one particular trait: as the ball approaches home plate, the seams of the baseball are spinning from the bottom upward—because, with the fastball, the ball is rolling off a pitcher's fingers, causing the ball to spin backward, toward the pitcher. The upward spin causes the ball to rise because air is flowing under the ball faster than it is flowing over the ball. This is the same principle that allows an airplane to fly. Most power pitchers throw their fastballs across the seams, and that's the fastball that will tend to rise most.

Facing a fastball thrown *with* the seams, you may notice how the ball will appear lighter in color, because you are seeing only two seams spin rather than all four. Although the spin of this pitch is still upward, it will be somewhat angular; the ball will move into a right-hander if thrown by a righty and away from him if thrown by a lefty. It won't rise as much as a fastball thrown across the seams.

Curveball

When the curveball is properly thrown, the spin is the opposite of that on a fastball, meaning the ball will sink, not rise. Downward spin is generated when the pitcher comes straight over the top on his release and pulls down on the ball, snapping his wrist sharply upon release.

If you look hard enough, you'll also notice the spin on the curve will be looser, more visible to the naked eye than that of the fastball. Why? Simple. You can't throw the pitch as hard. The difference you'll notice from a pitcher with a three-quarter release as opposed to one over the top is that rather than spinning straight downward, the curve will angle slightly across the plate. On a clock it would spin from the two o'clock position if thrown by a righty or the ten o'clock position if thrown by a lefty. This causes the ball to move not only down but also away from a righty if thrown by a righty.

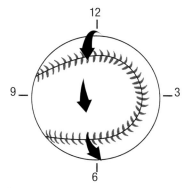

Overhand curveball. When properly thrown, spin is nearly twelve o'clock to six o'clock.

Notice the hand position of this lefty in comparison with his hand position in the photo on the facing page. Here, he's under the ball. He can throw a slider from this arm slot, but he'd need a higher arm slot to throw a good curve.

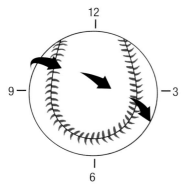

Slider. Tighter rotation and more revolutions than the curveball. Sharper sideways break toward four o'clock.

Slider

The slider is a tough pitch to judge because many pitchers throw it from different arm positions. The primary difference between the slider and the curve is that the slider has a tighter spin (faster revolutions) and a more sudden, more horizontal movement. Many players say that the combination of the tight, downward, cross-seam spin causes a small dot to form on the baseball where all fours seams meet—so look for that. It's just an optical illusion, and not all batters pick it up, but if you can, you'll find it easier to recognize the pitch. Another thing to remember about the slider is that it's moving quicker than a curveball but not quite as quick as a fastball. When thrown by a right-hander, the pitch will break 6 to 8 inches out and away from a right-handed hitter (or into a lefty). If thrown at belt level, it's a nice pitch to hit. But if it's coming in down and away, like the former World Series MVP Randy Johnson threw it, try to leave it alone, because by the time you get to it, chances are it will be out of the strike zone. Of course, if it's a borderline two-strike pitch, try to fight it off or hit it foul. A lot of times you're just not going to be able to hold up, and you're going to wind up swinging at a ball. Just accept it and be ready for the next one.

Split-Finger Fastball

The split-finger fastball achieved a certain cult status in the 1980s, thanks in part to the Hall of Fame success of Bruce Sutter and, later, students of Roger Craig (former manager of the Giants), such as Jack Morris and Dan Petry. Today, it's one of Roy Halladay's best strikeout pitches. The split-finger pitch is used as a change-of-pace pitch, even though it is actually quite fast, as little as five miles an hour slower than a fastball. This pitch looks like a slider, but there is no rotation on the ball. At the last instant, instead of moving horizontally, it suddenly drops. The best way to battle it is to stay back and not commit your hands until you're sure the pitch is going to stay in the strike zone. Try to get the barrel of the bat under this pitch so you hit it to the opposite field.

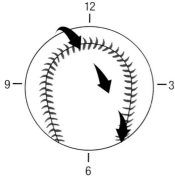

Split-finger fastball. Curveball-type spin with near-fastball velocity.

Change-Up

A good change should always be thrown off the fastball motion, with the same arm speed and the same release point, the only difference being velocity. There's also a variation of the change, the "circle change"—so named because it's thrown by encircling the ball between the thumb and forefinger. As the pitcher pulls down on the ball, you get the same spin as the fastball but little of the speed. (The pitch rarely climbs over 80 miles per hour on the radar gun.)

If you're anxious and trying to pull the change—especially if it's on the outside corner, where it belongs—all you'll hit are easy ground-outs. So wait and try to take it back up the middle or to the opposite field. Here too, keep the barrel of the bat under the ball. If the pitch is on the inner half of the plate, you can still pull it without swinging over the top.

Now what do you see? The reverse twisting of the pitcher's hand at release point tells me that this pitch is a screwball. It will tail away from a right-handed hitter and into a left-handed hitter.

This pitcher is about to release a change-up. His arm angle and release point are almost identical to those in the photo of the same pitcher's fastball release. (p. 62)

Can't Read Spin? Look for Location and Hand Position

Some people just don't have the eyesight or the ability to read spin. If you don't, look location. Pick up the ball upon its release and compute whether it's going to be inside, outside, high, low, or down the middle. Once you've come to some kind of decision, prepare yourself mentally—and mechanically—for a pitch in that spot. *But don't overcompensate.* That's the worst thing you can do. Anticipate, yes. But don't lean so much in one direction that you're helpless if the pitcher, say, misses the anticipated spot. It's all right to feel, on a 1-2 count, that the pitch will be coming inside, and to have the bat ready. But don't start leaning back or opening up before the ball reaches you. Be patient and concentrate.

Another helpful tool if you cannot read spin—or if you prefer not to look for location—is to look for the position of the pitcher's hand on the release point. More often than not, the position of a pitcher's hands and fingers will tell you just what pitch he's throwing you.

For instance, if the grip at release point has you seeing two fingers straight ahead, you know a fastball is coming. The fingers will face you at more or less a twelve o'clock position. When the fingers are facing you at a two o'clock position, there's a good chance that a cut fastball is on its way.

Oftentimes with a change-up you'll see four fingers pointing your way. The key to the change-up is that the pitcher's arm speed is the same as a fastball—or at least that's what he's trying to do. But upon the release point, you'll see four fingers rather than the two over the top that you would see with a fastball.

When the pitcher begins his throwing motion on the curveball, he will begin to pull down on the pitch—almost as if he's pulling down a string—an action that will become even more pronounced at the release point.

So if reading the spin isn't something for you, location is—whether you're looking for location on the pitch itself or beforehand for the location of the pitcher's fingers and hand on the release point.

I was fortunate enough to be able to read the spin of the ball. Spin told me what pitch to expect. Many people can't read spin, but if you are looking at the pitcher's release point, his hand position will tell you what pitch is coming. On page 61, this pitcher's grip at release has "change-up" written all over it—just as his two-finger straight-ahead release on this pitch tells me it's a fastball. Again, compare this pitch to the change-up and you'll see that his release point is exactly the same.

Making Adjustments

As I've said, if you're smart, you can learn to use your body to limit the strengths of opposing pitchers and force them to play your game. The key is automatically knowing, once you see a certain style of pitcher, how to handle him. Certainly you can, if you feel confident enough, match your best against his. But my advice is don't, on any occasion, say, crouch deeply in the box against a heralded curveballer just because someone tells you that's the best way to hit that type of pitcher. You know yourself better than anyone. You make the decisions. But before you do, take these specific situations into consideration.

Quick review . . . where are my eyes now? That's right, the pitcher has broken his hands, so my eyes are at the release point.

Hard thrower on the mound, coming over the top. When a pitcher comes over the top, his fastball rises and seems to pick up speed as it approaches the plate. Therefore, pitches up in the strike zone are easier to track but harder to hit. My adjustment in this situation is to crouch a bit to bring my strike zone down, in turn forcing the pitcher down—and thereby decreasing the rising movement on his fastball, theoretically making it easier for me to see and hit. That's one of the reasons I enjoyed success against Nolan Ryan over the years; I was able to take some heat off his fastball. I did the same with Mario Soto of Cincinnati in an All-Star Game one year. Mario had great stuff—a superb fastball combined with a devastating change-up. Well, in my mind it was important to close the miles-per-hour gap between his fastball and change, to make the pitches look more alike, reducing my chance of being fooled. I wanted to see his fastball early in the count, so I went into my crouch. Mario obliged, bringing his fastball down, lowering its speed—and its effectiveness. That, in turn, made his change a bit easier to detect.

Now, I know what you're thinking. Will the umpire buy this move? Absolutely. If an ump notices you're dropping down—as long as it's not ridiculously low—he's going to compensate in his crouch and go down with you. If he doesn't, don't be shy; mention it to him between innings, anywhere out of earshot of the pitcher or catcher.

Fastball pitcher, three-quarter motion. Basically, most pitchers who throw at three-quarter sidearm make more pitches that end up down in the strike zone than up. It's just the nature of their delivery; most of their pitches tend to sink. In this case, my preference was to crouch a bit, to see the ball longer.

Finally, I usually stood up straight in only two cases (this is how scientific one can get): against left-handers who come over the top and high-ball pitchers who don't have the "stuff" to overpower me up. Against lefties from the side, I crouched. My reasoning runs like this: Against over-the-top left-handers I was a much better high-ball hitter, so I stayed up. Lefties who came from the side gave me trouble when upright, so I dropped down to get better visibility on the pitch.

And now a word or two about stance and slump. I think most hitters think that when they're in a slump they need a complete overhaul instead of looking carefully for a small cause. In my case, I left my stance alone, getting a little more aggressive with my hands and, again, staying on the same plane as the ball. The stance is the base from which your entire game is built. Take your time finding the right one(s), but when you do, stick with it (them).

Follow every pitch you take into the catcher's glove and make a mental note of what that pitcher threw you at what point in the count. Pitchers develop patterns. Just make sure you never guess on a pitch. Look for a fastball and adjust for those change-ups, curveballs, screwballs, and knuckle balls.

Chapter 4

Contact!

Shoot for a rhythmic glide into an aggressive swing.

The analogy may seem a bit bizarre, but to become a dangerous presence at the plate, you need to add some music to your life. At times the music must be hot, aggressive, as when the hands drive through the strike zone, attacking the baseball. Other times, as during the glide that sets up the swing, a softer, more delicate approach is necessary. Mess up this harmony—make a heavy-metal movement when easy listening will do—and you'll find yourself hitting nothing but a lot of sour notes. Therefore, your goals as a hitter should be simple and direct. Make solid, consistently crisp contact. No excess movements, no complicated formulas. Just get the bat head into the proper position to drive through the contact zone.

The entire hitting process begins, quite naturally, when you step into the batter's box. Some players like to dig a hole under their back foot because that's comfortable for them. I preferred to cover up any holes or ruts so that the ground in the batter's box was level beneath my feet. This allowed me to settle in easily and inconspicuously. When you decide where to stand (for me it was the back inside edge of the batter's box), make sure you have proper plate coverage. Your bat needs to be able to reach pitches that are at least two inches off the outside corner of the plate.

Both my legs were always in a flexible position and my weight was always centered under me. This allowed me to make my first move away from the pitch once it was being

Opposite page: Your goals as a hitter should be simple and direct: make solid, consistently crisp contact.
Tony Tomsil/Getty Images

Vision: each player has a dominant eye. To determine your dominant eye, look into a camera or a microscope. The eye that you select to look through your eyepiece is your dominant eye. Most right-handers are right-eye dominant, and most lefties are left-eye dominant. Tony Gwynn and I were left-handed hitters who were right-eye dominant. It was an advantage. I recommend that hitters' heads face the mound to get your dominant eye as close to the pitcher as possible.

delivered, getting into my launch position. At that point, my hands were held about letter-high, a foot or so away from my body. I held the bat loosely, free from tension. My bat was almost parallel to the ground, very flat. My reason for keeping the bat flat and near the letters was strictly personal—it was a comfortable place to start. What you want to avoid, however, are the extremes: hands held stationary well above the shoulder or down below the waist. Both contribute to increased unnecessary movement and long, looping swings, which limit reaction time and ultimately rob you of proper arm extension.

What you're shooting for next is crucial to good hitting: a rhythmic glide into the ball; a balanced, streamlined weight shift; and an aggressive, hand-driven swing. You can't be stationary and expect to hit well; you lose too much flexibility and consistency. With this in mind, here's a step-by-step breakdown of one swing that's been a rather big hit over the years.

Here's a sequence where the hitter has put all the elements of a good swing together for solid contact. He starts with his weight centered, has a nice short stride, his bat is on the same plane as the ball, his hands are flat, his back foot has pivoted, arms are extended, contact is in front of the plate, he hits through the ball, and has a great finish.

Step 1: The Setup

Watch the pitcher. Don't stare a hole through him, but remember what you've learned about focusing on the release point and reading the spin. As the pitcher begins to come out of his motion, your hands should drop downward and toward the waist, beginning your rhythm. Then bring them back up, taking your bat from the previous flat position into a 90-degree angle behind the head (a place, incidentally, at which many players begin their stroke). This process releases some tension and started me into the rhythm of the one-piece swing. It is a pendulum-like effect. Swing down, swing up, never resting at any point in the arc. The eyes, in this situation, never leave the pitcher's hand; the head is relaxed, resting on the front shoulder. You want both eyes facing the pitcher, so turn your

Weight transfer is critical to a good swing. You need to load your weight on your back leg and use the energy generated by the weight transfer as you stride into the ball.

head—not too far—until you've gained full vision. Each person has a dominant eye—one eye that is stronger than the other. In most cases right-handers are right-eye dominant and left-handers are left-eye dominant. The reason I bring that up is because, in most cases, your weaker eye is the eye that's closest to the pitcher and thus gets the first look at the ball. That is why it's important to get both eyes as square to the pitcher as possible. Bring that dominant eye into play as much as possible.

Now, as the pitcher is about to release the ball, remember: the bat should be in a ready position, hands and weight centered. Your back side (left side for lefty, right for righty) should remain vertical, near 90 degrees, not tilting at the waist.

Step 2: The Stride

The purposes of the stride are varied: it gets your energies moving in the right direction, eliminates a flat-footed swing, balances the weight shift, and decreases tension. So how do you find the right stride? As with so many other things, you experiment. We all tend to gravitate to what's comfortable, so keep that in mind during batting practice. Use different strides, short and long, and see what best suits your body type. It's important that you don't overstride, as it could cause you to get your weight out front, and to be a good hitter you need to stay back. For my money, a short stride (about 4 to 6 inches) is best. A longer stride generally limits your flexibility, has a tendency to pull your hands or torso too far forward, and forces you to lunge after the ball. Remember, you can make big strides as a hitter without *taking* them. Harmon Killebrew, a former teammate and a Hall of Famer on and off the field, did. He hit 573 career home runs (an average of 1 every 14 at bats, fifth on the all-time list), and Harmon, for a big man, had one of the shortest strides I've ever seen. More recently, Cardinals and Angels all-star Jim Edmonds had a great career—four-time all-star, nearly 400 home runs, and 1,200 RBI—with virtually no stride.

We had Jim Edmonds start with his weight centered and then, when the pitch was delivered and without picking up his foot, shift his weight backwards before finally unleashing his torque through the swing. This no-stride approach is not for everyone, but it worked for Jim. *John Biever/Sports Illustrated/Getty Images*

Stride and Pivot: Your front foot should always step toward the pitcher, whether your stance is open or closed. As you stride and swing, it's critical to use your back foot to pivot as you start your hands through the hitting zone, so it is in the same position as shown in this photo. I prefer a shorter stride of about 4 to 6 inches.

Note the position of this player's back foot. He made a nice stride, but his failure to finish the pivot with his back foot sucked the energy out of his swing.

Now, once you decide on a stride, don't change it. You may decide, depending on the pitcher, to set up in different areas of the batter's box, but your stride should always be in the same direction—right back at the pitcher. And no matter what stance I took, the length of the stride never varied, and my front toe always pointed down at a 45-degree angle. With an angled front toe you eliminate the tendency to open up too quickly with your hips, forcing your front shoulder to open and the head and eyes to follow. If you're doing your mechanics properly, the hips, shoulders, and head should open naturally, forcing your hands through the strike zone. By the time your front foot hits, the ball is halfway to home plate and you will have made a decision on whether to swing or take the pitch. If you take it, just keep the hands back and follow the ball into the catcher's glove. But if you decide to swing, well, that's when your hands have to go to work.

Step 3: Flat-Hand Hitting

If any single idea dominates my approach to hitting, it would be my undying belief in the advantages of flat-hand hitting. The advantages are these: increased *flexibility* to react to a variety of pitches; more *leverage* in driving the baseball; better *arm extension*; ability to get the *bat and ball on the same plane*; a later, more natural *rolling of the wrists*; and the ability to *wait longer* on any pitch.

This is an example of flat-hand hitting. As your bat comes through the zone, the palm of your top hand faces up, while the palm of your bottom hand faces the ground.

There are a lot of good things going on in this photo, not the least of which are his flat hands. Flat hands help your swing get maximum arm extension. Still, I'd like to see his head more on the ball, and the contact point should be a bit more out front.

Don't be a top-hand hitter. See how the thumb has rolled over as the bat passes through the hitting zone? Rolling your top hand too quickly causes you to get all tied up inside and takes away all your arm extension. Once in a while you can time the rolling hands with the incoming pitch and drive the ball; however, the result is usually a weak pop fly or a ground ball.

Flat-hand hitting is a term directly opposed to the often-taught method of top-hand hitting, or rolling your wrists as the ball and bat come together. Fundamentally, instead of having the fingertips of your top hand pointing to the sky—as they would be if your hands were flat—your top-hand thumb is down, the fingertips either facing downward or pointed at the pitcher. But as you will see—and this is important—flat-hand hitting does not mean the bat never leaves a horizontal plane. On the contrary, *the angle of the bat adjusts with the location of the pitch. The location of the pitch, in turn, dictates when the hands are released.*

Your back elbow is a key to flat-hand hitting. It ignites the swing, flattening out your hands automatically. Try it. Stand up with an imaginary bat. Get your bat in the eleven o'clock position. Now pull down with your back elbow. The fingertips on the top hand should begin to point skyward, the bat moving, as you swing, toward horizontal.

You must remember that to become a threat at the plate, both hands must work for you. In this sequence the bottom hand works with the back elbow to pull the hands through the strike zone. The role of the top hand is most often to "quicken" the stroke, to help direct the bat head on the proper angle to the baseball. The back wrist in this flat-handed position remains cocked. Keeping it cocked forces your hands farther in front of the bat head, and on every pitch except those thrown inside, you want your hands to lead the swing. Okay, now we're in an optimum hitting position— hands flat, wrists cocked, head stationary, weight shifted, arms beginning to extend. What next? It all depends on the pitch.

Inside Pitch

Whether it's a fastball or an off-speed pitch, the basic stride-swing fundamentals don't change; only the release of the hands changes. By "release" I mean making a conscious decision to go after the pitch, to fire the bat at the ball. And I do mean fire. You can't baby your hands through the contact zone. Take a rip! Be aggressive. React. When a ball is bearing down inside or in the middle of the plate, you want to commit your hands earlier than when the pitch is on the outside part of the plate. Doing so gets your hands, and thus the bat head, through the contact zone sooner, allowing you to get your hips quickly into the swing. But don't get careless. Stay on balance and remain composed. And once that light inside your brain flashes the word "swing," be ready to explode at the baseball.

Now, at contact on the pitch inside, the barrel of your bat should be parallel with your hands. If you're doing things really right, the barrel should be beyond home plate.

Okay, so we know how and at what point to hit the ball. Now let's make sure we hit it. Ego is a strong emotional force, and it works for—and against—all of us in life. In baseball we all want to hit home runs. Face it: we'd all love to hit like Ruth, Aaron, Griffey Jr., or Barry Bonds. Some say there's no bigger thrill than jogging around the bases, the crowd chanting your name. And, truth be told, it's hard to beat. But not all of us—in fact, very few

You must remember that to become a threat at the plate, both hands must work for you.

The contact zone for hitting is always in front of home plate. How far out front you hit the ball will determine how much you pull the ball, and pitch location will determine how far in front of the plate you hit the ball.

of us—are born home-run hitters. We don't possess the size, the strength, or the raw power to play home-run derby successfully. I can't tell you how many times in my career I've seen a situation where a single would win a game and some big lug was up at the plate, swinging like there was no tomorrow.

It's the same sad song in Little League: so many big swings and so little contact, with style winning out over substance. So if you're consistently striking out or missing pitches, dial down a bit on the swing. Concentrate on contact.

Finally, imagine writing a symphony and forgetting the last movement. Like any artist, if you quit before you've finished—for us, before contact—you've stopped just short of success. Therefore, as a line-drive hitter, a gap hitter, it's crucial to remember to follow through upon contact, extending your arms and the bat head. It's the only way I know that we small guys can compete with the bigger hitters.

A Pitch over the Middle or Outside

The key here is to delay the wrist release in relation to how far the ball is from the middle of home plate. The farther outside the ball is, the longer you can wait. But the approach doesn't differ: the wrists still move into the pitch in a cocked position, hands flat, head still. Force yourself to wait, to delay committing to the ball, until the pitch has entered the contact zone. Often now, because of my practice and experience, I can wait until the pitch is just a few feet from home plate before I fire my hands at the ball, knowing that all the other mechanics are in place, the weight shifted, head steady.

It's important to get your bat on the same plane as the ball. You want to be able to swing down on a ball that is up in the zone, and uppercut a ball down in the zone.

With an outside pitch, your hands must get ahead of the bat head. If the pitch is down, you want the barrel of the bat below it. You don't have to try to overpower the pitch; just concentrate on contact. You'll be shocked how quickly the ball travels into an infield hole or an outfield gap. And hit the ball where it's pitched; don't pull a pitch that has "opposite field" written all over it or you'll wind up hitting weak ground balls.

Hitting the Breaking Ball

This is the bane of almost every hitter. The key to hitting the curve is deciding where the ball is headed and *being patient* enough to let it get there. The major difference in adjustment to inside and outside curves is in where the ball contacts the bat. The ideal contact point on the bat, whatever the pitch, is the sweet spot, as shown in the illustration on page 30.

Don't lunge after a breaking ball. Let it come to you and explode at the ball.

With breaking pitches, hand quickness is paramount to get the bat head on the ball—but patience is a virtue. Keep your heel planted to avoid lunging after a pitch. Let it come to you. Then explode at the ball. The longer you can keep your hands back, your head still, and your body in balance, the better, more consistent contact you'll make. Remember: let the ball come to you before you make your move.

Finally, fastball or curve, inside or out, I realize your initial reaction, when thinking about rhythm, stride, and swing, will be to swing in steps: one . . . two . . . three. But hitting isn't square dancing or field-goal kicking. You can't take the hands back . . . then step . . . then swing. It takes too much time; the result will not be instinctive or reactive, but laborious and mechanical. You must strive for—and believe me, it's not easy—three distinct movements meshed into one, the separate movements distinguishable perhaps to a slow-motion video camera but seen as a single component by the naked eye.

The Upper Half

What's going on upstairs, with the torso and shoulders, while our hands are working overtime? Ideally, not too much. The less movement the better; you don't want to disturb an otherwise balanced, rhythmic stride and swing. One important point, though: remember to move your head *down* with the pitch. I can't emphasize enough the importance of eliminating excess head movement, of keeping that head down and tucked. Move it and your shoulders pull out, and you lose critical balance and control.

Obviously, another benefit of keeping your head down is allowing you to "see" the bat hit the ball. But can you really see it? I don't think so. Sometimes, though, when you're really in the groove, it seems as though you can, even though closing your eyes for a split second upon contact is a natural, instinctive, involuntary reaction. What you have to do is work to keep your eyes open and on the ball as long as you can. One of the big problems with .250 hitters is that they may see the ball fine out of the hand, but they lose sight of the pitch over the last 3 feet. They're "57 1/2-foot hitters," groping and guessing where the pitch is headed, an unfortunate situation because so much of the movement on a fastball, curve, or slider comes so late, often in those last 3 feet. You'll find the longer you keep your head down and your eyes open, the better contact you'll make.

The Bottom Half

The truth is, the bottom part of your body—the legs and hips—is the better half when it comes to hitting a baseball. Unfortunately, many players, particularly young ones, neglect it. Yes, I can see you in the weight rooms now, muscling up on the machines, thinking the bigger you are upstairs, the better a hitter you'll be. Not so. True, muscles and strength are important, but get too pumped up and you'll find your fluid stride, your rhythm, all out of sync, unable to produce the long ball—more than likely the reason you started lifting weights in the first place. Instead, concentrate on good mechanics and a quick swing and you'll find yourself driving the ball, no matter what your size.

But back to the bottom half. In every swing it's important that your body stay squarely balanced, turning tightly, as if a pole were running from the top of your cap through the middle of your body, and you rotate on this axis. The hips should open naturally with the swing, the rotation squarely in the direction of the pitcher. What you want to guard against—and this is something all players fall prey to from time to time—is opening up too soon. This causes an immediate chain reaction, pulling out your front shoulder, taking your torso, arms, head, and everything else imaginable off the ball. What remains is a leaning tower, unbalanced, useless. And what about the back leg? Here are two points: When contact is made, the back leg, from the foot to the hip, should be angled, with the toes turned toward the pitcher. The heel is up off the ground. This movement facilitates proper hip rotation; it keeps the entire body in one tight, vertical alignment, a prerequisite to a powerful stroke.

To Uppercut or Not to Uppercut

Because the baseball generally comes to home plate on a downward path, many hitters feel compelled to compensate by swinging up on the baseball to "level out" the pitch. Not me. Uppercutting has really only one place in my baseball book: when your team needs a sacrifice fly and you must lift the ball to the outfield. In that case, it's okay to uppercut certain pitches. Otherwise, I don't believe in it. Here's why: it's very likely most of your hits will be airborne, and lofted fly balls make the easiest outs. Uppercutting also creates difficulty in getting the arms fully extended and your weight properly transferred—keys to solid contact. Even more important, it causes the collapse of the rear leg and shoulder, which in turn causes the batter to tilt backward, raising the front shoulder and opening the front hip too early. It also brings the hands and bat down to an ineffective position.

When a person suffers from uppercutting, it's often because he collapses his back shoulder too soon. As I said, you need to move your weight forward when you stride. By taking the weight off the back leg and transferring it forward, you'll cure any problems associated with uppercutting. Of course, not every pitch is perfect, every fastball belt-high, every swing level. Consequently, as hitters, we must be able to adjust to pitches that are a shade too high or too low, ones that require us occasionally to take imperfect cuts. At least with ground balls you're giving yourself half a chance. With the advent of artificial turf, with dirt infields known for a bad hop or two, and given the fact that fielders must first catch and then throw the baseball, ground balls simply make for tougher plays. I have a similar theory for "dead pull" hitters. I'm not against pulling the ball. If you have the ability, fine. But what I've found is that by pulling every ball, you narrow your hitting area by one half or more. You also get into situations against pitchers you have no business trying to pull.

Avoiding Infield Pop-Ups

Toward the latter part of 1985, Wade Boggs, then of the Red Sox, received some well-deserved national attention. For the most part it focused on the fact that he had finished the season with 240 hits, one more than I had in 1977, which, until Boggs surpassed it, was the most by any hitter since 1930. The statistic that caught many an eye, however, was this: Boggs went almost the entire season (until September) before he popped out to the infield. Well, I don't know if that stat was ever kept on me, but I doubt that I popped out to an infielder even 50 times in 20 years, and, as with Boggs, there are several reasons. First of all, neither of us was very interested in hitting the bottom half of the baseball. We consciously tried to hit the middle half or the top half, and we also had the discipline to lay off high or rising pitches that are made for popping up.

Flat-handed hitting acts as a deterrent to hitting infield pop-ups.

Additionally, Boggs and I didn't uppercut on the ball unless, as I've said, we were in a situation that called for us to hit a sacrifice fly to the outfield. That's one reason you like to have a Ryan Howard at the plate if you need a fly ball. Ryan's stroke is an uppercut swing that's primed for power. He hits a lot of long fly balls, but he also pops up to the infield quite a bit. That's one of the benefits of flat-hand hitting. It acts as a deterrent to hitting pop flies to the infield, because by the sheer mechanics of the swing it forces you to use the whole bat, keeping it steady as you drive through the baseball. In top-hand hitting you are rolling the bat in a downward motion, thus exposing the top half of the bat, in effect compounding the problem of making contact because the bat is moving not only forward but downward. Even with a level arm movement, unless you hit the ball perfectly, you're most likely going to pop the ball up, pull it foul, or miss it entirely.

What also causes pop-ups to the infield is waiting too long to pull the trigger—not exploding at a pitch you want to hit. Through indecisiveness, a hitter can "jam" himself with a pitch—wait until the ball is too deep in the contact zone and you're going to get jammed and never get the barrel of the bat on the ball. If you are fortunate enough to make contact on the narrow part of the bat, there just isn't enough wood there to get the ball into the outfield.

Up the Middle/Opposite Field

> **The best way to earn respect as a hitter is to learn to hit the ball up the middle.**

The best way to earn respect as a hitter is to learn to hit the ball up the middle. I know, I know: easier said than done. I realize that most of you are not professionals and that in Little League or high school practices are brief and attention spans short. There are more pressing priorities than hitting 200 balls right back at the pitcher. But there's only one way that's going to change, and that's with practice. Hard, sweaty, serious practice. Eventually that practice will pay off, just as it did for me in the third inning on August 4, 1985. I was facing Frank Viola of Minnesota and was one hit shy of becoming only the sixteenth man in baseball history to record 3,000 career hits. At 1:47 p.m., Viola threw a 1-1 slider, and I flared a soft line drive into short left field. Afterward, my teammate Bob Boone mentioned how appropriate the location of that historic hit was. "It wouldn't have been right had it been any other type of hit," he said. The implication was obvious: Of my 3,000-plus career hits, hundreds went to what I call "My Favorite Spot."

And just exactly where is this garden spot? For a left-handed hitter, it's a large area that starts about 5 feet to the hitter's right of second base and extends all the way to the left-field line. For a righty, the area shifts from just to the left of second base to

This hitter puts a great swing on a pitch he is hitting the other way. Notice how he has adjusted his swing to drop the barrel of the bat below his hands to get his bat on the same plane as the ball. He keeps his weight and his hands back on this ball. His finish has all his momentum moving in the direction of the hit.

the right-field line. And why is it so rewarding? Well, up the middle/opposite field is nice because it allows for mistakes, for miscalculations. If you're a lefty, say, and always aiming for that spot (except in specific situations, which we'll discuss in Chapter 7), and on a given pitch you're off a bit, the ball can still fall in front of the center fielder or left fielder, skip past the shortstop, go over second base, or bounce off the pitcher for a hit. So remember this phrase: up the middle/opposite field. Recite it. Burn it inside your head. Tony Gywnn did, and he's in the Hall of Fame. Ichiro and Derek Jeter do, and they are on their way, too. Learn to contact the ball and drive it there (with adjustments, of course, for inside pitches), and you'll go a long way as a hitter.

Contact in the Strike Zone: Hit the Ball Where It's Pitched

We just spent a long chapter discussing and illustrating how to make good contact. Now let's put those lessons into application as they pertain to the strike zone.

The official rules of Major League Baseball define the strike zone as follows: "The strike zone is that area over home plate the upper limit of which is a horizontal line at the midpoint between the top of the shoulders and the top of the uniform pants, and the lower level is a line at the hollow beneath the kneecap. The Strike Zone shall be determined from the batter's stance as the batter is prepared to swing at a pitched ball."

While the strike zone is constant (subject to umpire interpretation), every batter's hitting zone is different. Ted Williams published an illustration that linked batting averages to pitches delivered into certain areas of the strike zone. Ted was one of the greatest hitters ever, but he and I never agreed when it comes to his strike-zone theory. Ted's illustration was fine as it related to Ted, but there were pitches in Ted's chart where, when he hit .275, I hit .330, and vice versa. Hall of Famer Yogi Berra was a notorious bad-ball hitter and he won three American League MVP Awards. More recently, Vlad Guerrero's hitting zone could be defined as any ball that leaves the pitcher's

Here is the basic strike zone. As per the rules of baseball, the strike zone extends vertically from the edges of home plate, intersecting at the knees and letters of the uniform.

I divide the strike zone into four quarters and add a sweet spot down the middle. Zones 1 and 2 are high strikes, while 3 and 4 are low strikes.

This ball in Zone 1 is high and away in the strike zone. The hitter needs to drive this ball to the area between left-center and right-center. To do so he needs to get good extension of his hands and stay on top of the ball. If he tries to uppercut this pitch, he will fly out.

hand and reaches home plate—and a few that one-hop it. Players must identify their hitting zones and learn to hit the ball where it's pitched. Ted Williams's was almost exclusively a pull hitter, and he still hit .344 for his career. I can only wonder what Ted would have hit had he used the entire field and hit the ball where it was pitched.

Trust me, you don't have Ted Williams's skill. For players like you, me, Tony Gwynn, Ichiro, Robbie Canó, Joe Mauer, and Adrian Gonzalez, we need to use the whole field from foul pole to foul pole. You do that by hitting the ball where it's pitched. Let me show you what I mean.

If you can hit a pitch outside the strike zone that you can drive, go for it. Be aggressive, but stay disciplined. Just remember the mechanics for hitting pitches in proximity to the appropriate quadrant of the strike zone. You will also want to use these mechanics when you have two strikes and you don't want to take a called strike three. Spoiling pitches is an art. If you can't handle a pitch down and away, especially if it is a breaking ball, learn to foul it into the first-base dugout and live to see another pitch. Foul off enough pitches and you just might see a discouraged pitcher serve you up something right down the middle.

This pitch in Zone 2 is a strike up and on the inside quarter of the strike zone. This ball needs to be hit between left-center and the left-field foul pole. As with the ball in Zone 1, the hitter needs to stay on top of the ball and drive through contact, hitting the ball well in front of home plate. A key to hitting this pitch is to keep your front shoulder in. Make sure you don't allow your front shoulder or your hips to fly open too quickly, or the head of your bat will lag behind your hands.

This pitch down and away in Zone 3 should be hit into the area between right-center and the right-field foul pole. It's a pitch that will require you to flex your knees (which will allow you to see the ball better) and to drop the barrel of the bat lower than your hands as you drive through the pitch. Derek Jeter has made a living on this pitch by keeping his hands inside the ball and letting the ball get closer to home plate. You are not Derek Jeter, so you may not want to wait as long on this pitch as he does, but get the barrel of your bat down to the ball, take a good swing, and you will get your hits.

You should be looking to hit this pitch in Zone 4 between left field and the left-field foul pole. You want to get to this pitch a little farther out in front of the plate, and you want to adjust your lower body to get your bat on the same plane as the ball. Again, don't try to uppercut this pitch, especially if you are a stand-up hitter.

The sweet spot. You will only see a ball here when the pitcher makes a mistake. I haven't played Major League Baseball in more than 25 years, but feed me a diet of balls in the sweet spot and I can still hit .300. Just see this ball and put your best swing on it. Your eyes will light up when you recognize a ball in this zone. Just don't get overanxious; stay composed and hit it hard.

Ted Williams was one of the greatest hitters of all time. We had a great deal of respect for each other and talked hitting often, agreeing on most things. One thing Ted and I never agreed on was pitch selection within the strike zone. *Tony Triolo/Sports Illustrated/Getty Images*

I can practice hitting the ball where it's pitched using the tee. Here's that same ball in Zone 4 from the left side.

Chapter 5

The Mental Game

**Do you believe
you're an all-star
or an also-ran?**

So much of baseball is played inside the head. It's a silent fight waged not before a crowd, in public view, but rather in darkness, in hotel rooms or locker rooms, a battle between the forces of self-doubt and dogged determination. And it is the losers of those battles who so often speak of a lack of confidence, an innate fear of playing under pressure.

There are, in my mind, two kinds of confidence that affect performance at the plate. The first kind deals with the ability to overcome outside influences, having a strong enough character to deal with negative press, overbearing fans and coaches—you name it. The other, more subtle type of confidence deals with how *you* perceive yourself as a player. Do *you* believe you're an all-star or an also-ran? If you give the latter answer to this question, your play on the field will reflect it. But when you've learned to shut off outside influences and believe in yourself, there's no telling how good a player you can be. That's because you've got the mental edge. When you have that edge, when you feel it, no pitcher is too tough, no worry worth sweating. Lose it, however, and see how quickly the game changes. Hits stop falling. Worries increase. Excuses multiply. The lesson is, if you don't have confidence in yourself as a hitter, if you don't believe you're good, no book on hitting will make a difference.

First, let's take a look at overcoming outside influences, the most common—yet easiest—problem to control. I always advocate

Hitting a baseball requires tremendous focus and confidence. Step up to bat with the belief that you'll get a hit each and every time.

making rational decisions before taking any action. Don't do anything rash. Seek counsel from a coach, a parent, a pastor—don't let it burn inside you. Remember, you're going to have bad days. You're going to make errors. People are going to boo. Don't compound the problem by making obscene gestures or tasteless remarks. As soon as you give credence to outside influences, the situation only gets worse. So walk away and let your bat and glove do the talking. Of course—and I say this cautiously—there does come a time when you have to make a stand and fight for what's right. Just think before acting—that's all.

I found out about booing firsthand in 1974 when I led the league in errors at second base with 33. I can't count the number of times I wanted to crawl under the bag and disappear. Often my frustrations over being unmercifully booed—even though I was hitting well—spilled out in the locker room. One day it caught up with me. After a particularly difficult day I said something like, "Man, it sure would be nice to have a change." That, in turn, was twisted by a newspaperman into a trade request that read in the paper "Carew Wants to Be Traded." So be careful. The press can be very positive and well-meaning most of the time, but face it, you've got to be careful about what comes out of your mouth.

Pressures

In 1985 I experienced more outside pressure than most players feel in a lifetime. The pressure of becoming only the sixteenth player in history to record 3,000 hits was frightening, particularly because of the growing specter of a players' strike. I didn't want to wait until it was settled to pursue the milestone, because, in truth, the way things looked for a time, I didn't know if it would ever be settled.

So this time I learned from my experiences in 1977, the year I almost hit .400 (I finished at .388). That year, no matter where I went, the scene never varied: tape recorders in the face, phone calls at the hotel. We had to change our telephone number every two weeks. And always the same questions over and over: "Are you going to hit .400?" "What are you doing differently?" "Why are you hitting so well?"

I learned then that I shouldn't allow myself to go through that grind again. I decided that even though 3,000 hits was a major milestone, I was going to shut myself off from reporters, do what I had to do, because in 1977 the pressure had affected not only my fielding, but also my base running, my concentration, everything. I know that sounds like a harsh decision, and certainly among the press it was an unpopular one. Celebrity is wonderful, but without on-field performance you have no claim to celebrity.

> **We all want to start, to make all-star teams, to please our coaches, parents, scouts. But first we have to please ourselves.**

You will be evaluated throughout your career. Remember, those evaluations are only as good as the people making them. I didn't play baseball in high school, and Michael Jordan was cut from his high school basketball team as a sophomore. Stay relaxed when you are being evaluated. No matter the outcome, believe in your own ability and keep working hard.

Now, how does pressure reach down from the major league level into college, high school, even Little League? Easily. We all want to start, to make all-star teams, to please our coaches, parents, scouts. But first we have to please ourselves. We have to feel good about the effort, have the confidence that if given the opportunity, we'll perform.

So work and learn to believe in yourself, even if you don't get that precious college scholarship. Get a job; try out; find some way to play ball if that's what is important to you. Whether or not you get that scholarship is not entirely in your hands. During my high school years at George Washington in the Bronx, I played sandlot baseball in the Bronx Federation League, a tough, well-scouted circuit. One day the director of the Minnesota Twins farm system came to see me play. Was I nervous! This was my big chance. But you have to settle down. If scouts are in the stands, forget them; keep your mind on the game and concentrate on doing the little things right, being sound fundamentally. Use two hands during warmups; hustle. Give off a glow that says, "I love this game." And be careful how you dress. Personally, I'm a neatnik; my uniform had to be clean at all times. If it got dirty, I changed it. You, however, may have your own style of play, more Charlie Hustle, more down and dirty than me. That's fine. But don't look sloppy. A dirty uniform is one thing; a shirttail hanging out, silly hats during pre-game warmups, and droopy pants are quite another. Scouts have a sixth sense about this attitude, so clean or dirty, play like you mean it. By the way, the day the scout came to see me, we were playing on a field adjacent to Yankee Stadium. I was 9 for 10 in a doubleheader and hit 4 home runs.

Still, with all this effort, I'm a big believer in balancing the scales, in cultivating off-field hobbies and interests to draw your mind away from these pressures. You can't think baseball, football, whatever, 24 hours a day. You need a private life, a release. And if you're still in school, you need to know the books come first. You need a safety net, career opportunities, in case, for whatever reason, you don't make it to the big leagues. After all, how many players do? And don't be blinded by hero worship. To me, it's great to have young kids look up to athletes, movie stars, famous people, but take a look in another direction once in a while—to your teachers and, most importantly, your parents.

Finally, unfortunately, you'll find as you get older that time just naturally becomes your enemy. When I was younger, in my teens and early twenties, my confidence soared; I knew I could hit. But at 40 I realized my days of chasing a .400 average were over; I was never again going to average .354 over six seasons as

Speaking of education, here is the reality: You are most probably *not* going to play in the big leagues. When you get to high school and college, your at bats will be a privilege earned in the classroom. Knowledge is power, so do your homework and get good grades. You want to be a .300 hitter in life when your playing career is over.

What goes through your mind when you are on deck? You should be reading the pitcher and the game situation so you have a firm idea of what your approach to this at bat will be when it's your turn to hit.

I did from 1973 through 1978. Father Time starts fighting back. But still, I learned to live with him and adjust, not to try to play beyond my abilities, not to attack pitches at 40 the same way I did at 20. In short, I learned to play within my limitations, whatever they may have been.

One question often asked is "What happens if I'm drafted by the pros?" My advice, unless the money is extraordinary, is to go to college. If you're smart and have the desire for a life after baseball, get your degree. Quite honestly, college baseball today is just like a good minor-league experience—great coaching, travel, a World Series possibility, and 100-game schedules. If you're good enough to start at that level, don't worry; you'll get your chance to become a professional.

The second form of confidence is more difficult to develop. Of course, some people are seemingly born with a special gleam in their eye, a swagger to their step: Pete Rose, Don Mattingly, Ken Griffey Jr. For others, the mental edge is gained slowly; bit by bit, they grow into their greatness. Growing up, I *knew* I was going to be a good hitter. I woke up every morning telling myself, "You're the best there is." Don't be afraid to say it, to *believe* it. If you don't, nobody else will.

Certainly, part of this confidence quotient comes from knowing the game, knowing that a pitcher tends to tire in the sixth inning or that a certain outfielder's arm is weak. Putting this knowledge together with their superior skills helped players like Rose and Griffey win many a ballgame. Knowing they had an edge gave them the confidence to take advantage of it.

Focus on the game, even when you're not *in* the game. *Shutterstock*

The mental edge is not something you can buy or are born with. It begins long before you step into the batter's box. As I said, it means eating right, using the right equipment, knowing what you want to do at the plate with each pitcher you face. But it's also an attitude. A pitcher-be-damned, "I'm the best hitter you're going to face today or any other day" frame of mind that begins before you ever walk up to the plate. An attitude that says, "You've got a load on your hands, buddy, and the last name is Carew," one that stems from the simple phrase "I'm going to get a hit." Every time I walked up to home plate, no matter what happened previously, whether I was 0 for 20 or 5 for 5, I was going to get a hit. If I went up to home plate the first three times and got three singles, I wanted four singles. I was never complacent. I never said, "Ah, what the heck. I've got four; who needs five?" *I* needed five. And so do you. But with this confidence must also come discipline. Not the discipline espoused by Ted Williams, who said, "If you want to hit .300, you can only attack certain balls in certain zones." I made a living hitting balls out of the strike zone; in fact, I hit far more pitches out of the strike zone than down the middle. So, if you think you can handle a so-called ball, take a rip, especially if you know exactly what you want to do with that pitch. Some guys don't but swing anyway, compounding the problem by taking a mediocre pass at a somewhat bad pitch.

Still, so much has to do with what you *think* you can do, which directly relates to how you feel at the plate. In my mind, I'm in complete control in the box: composed, confident, quiet, concentrating on nothing but the task at hand. I put no outside pressure on myself—and that means, no matter how difficult it may be, not permitting personal problems to color my thinking. Unfortunately, this is easier said than done. Today, a lot of major league hitters walk up to home plate worrying about everything but hitting. Their contract. Their girlfriend. Their error in the previous inning. Even their Twitter account. The game's too tough for a distracted effort. If you bring outside pressure between the white lines, you're adding to your miseries. You almost have to be a machine out there, turned on when you come to the park, playing on something akin to automatic pilot. *You can get a hit anytime you want to, and you're going to get a hit.*

For you, the lesson to be learned and memorized, especially in youth, is not to compromise. Don't accept failure on *any* pitch. One player—young, very talented—succumbed for a short time. He'd sit on the bench befuddled, time and time again, by fastballs fed one after another on the outside of the plate. So what did he do? The worst possible thing. He started inching in, moving closer to the plate. Well, the next thing he knows, here comes the hard stuff—on the *inside* corner. So now he backs off. So they go back outside. Now he's *really* talking to himself.

If this player had practiced hitting the outside fastball over the course of a week or two, he would have put a stop to the problem. At the very least he would have seen hundreds of pitches in that trouble spot, and this would have helped him recognize the pitch, speed his reflexes, focus his attention on improving his hand–eye coordination. It took him a while, but that's what he finally did. So should you. Use a tee. Just set it up on the outside corner of the plate. Then concentrate, as if in a game, on every swing. You won't have to wait long to see the results.

The game's too tough for a distracted effort. If you bring outside pressure between the white lines, you're adding to your miseries.

Stay in every pitch of every at bat. Even when you take a pitch, follow the ball all the way into the catcher's glove. *Shutterstock*

Another common mental problem is how to handle a guy who always seems to have your number. No matter what you do, you can't seem to get a hit. I had that problem for years with Rudy May, the former New York Yankees left-hander. He *owned* me, principally because his motion (all arms and legs) was very confusing to me. My theory in this situation has always been to check your mechanics. I wasn't seeing the ball well, and I figured I had to make a mechanical adjustment. Well, I experimented for years—and I do mean years—without success. Finally, Rudy retired. Thank goodness! When this happens to you, your first adjustment should always be to run a mechanical check, opening your stance, closing it, waiting longer to take the outside pitch to right or left. The second adjustment is mental. You cannot say to yourself, "This pitcher is better than I am." Because as a hitter, *no* pitcher is better than you. *Nobody.* As soon as you give in to Mr. A, you'll find it easier to concede an at bat to Mr. B, then Mr. C. Pretty soon there's nobody left in the alphabet.

It's important to be a student of the game. There is no shortage of big-league games on TV. Watch baseball whenever you get the chance and see how the greats approach each at bat. You will find it very educational.

Slumps

Slumps are funny in how they can turn an otherwise well-adjusted human being into a frustrated, tentative creature. I've seen slumps make a perennial all-star selection change his stance every day. This player figured he could change his fundamental approach to a very difficult task and expect to get in a groove. Well, it didn't work. It can't work. It becomes more mental than physical.

Slumps are a part of the game, as indigenous to baseball as the national anthem and hot dogs. Play long enough and you'll stop hitting for a spell. What differentiates the better players from the rest is how they cope with temporary failure, no matter how exceedingly frustrating it is. Anybody who has played the game knows what I'm going to say. Hit a shot—a bullet—right at somebody, watch him catch it, and see how it feels. Or watch some infielder or outfielder pull a play out of his pants. My remedy for slumps is rather tried but still very true: a visit to the batting cage. But only a short visit—10 or 15 minutes a day. That's it. Work on what you want to work

Never throw the bat or equipment. First of all, it's bad sportsmanship. But just as importantly, it's showing the pitcher that he got inside your head. You are going to make outs 7 of 10 times. Never let the pitcher see you sweat. Get him next time.

on and get out. If you stay longer, you get sore or lazy, falling right back into your bad habits.

Also, don't attempt any major overhauls when a little fine-tuning will do. I think changing everything is the worst possible decision, especially if you're hitting in poor luck. If, however, you're continually popping pitches up or, worse, missing them, go to the videotape (that's the best way to detect mistakes) or have a *knowledgeable* coach watch your swing. You may be pulling off the ball; maybe your hands are lazy; maybe your back leg and shoulder are collapsing; but if you—via videotape—or a manager, coach, or teammate can spot these problems, all the better. Again, beware. Some managers have a good eye for hitting. Others do not. And though I think it's a coach's or teammate's duty to try to help, make sure that person has some track record or at least can speak intelligently about hitting. It's the same for you. If you see a teammate doing something new in the box, mention it. Don't belabor the point, but bring it up. I've had coaches who have seen me hit for years spot a tiny flaw, a new wrinkle in my swing. The next day I'm in the cage trying to iron it out. Also, coaches and teammates, offer some encouragement! If a guy in a slump hits a shot, speak up. A "good hit" or "nice stroke" goes a long way in boosting someone's sagging ego.

Another problem associated with a trip to rock bottom is a player's tendency to try to blast his way out of a slump. What's wrong with a bunt or two? Psychologically, it's a blessing, hitting a ball 30 feet for a single when dozens of long flies have been caught. You can always try to drop a bunt down, even when you're swinging the bat well. Why not?

Ultimately, though, slumping comes down to a state of mind. Let it eat at you and, many times, there'll be nothing left. This is where confidence *and* discipline really come to bat. You must discipline yourself to abide by the 10 keys to good hitting that I address in the introduction to this book. Relax and try not to force it, and remain confident in your abilities—even if no one else is.

Slumps are a part of the game. Don't make any major changes to your swing when you are in a slump. Sometimes it only takes one hit to break the slump, so consider laying down a bunt. It will look like a line drive in the box score.

The Confrontation

Like it or not, boiled down to its lowest common denominator, baseball is a numbers game. As a player you are constantly judged by the number of hits, runs, and RBI you accumulate, how you fare in what can be called "the confrontation." This individual battle between the pitcher and hitter occurs dozens of times each game; it's the heartbeat of any baseball game, and to improve you must acknowledge the importance of being mentally prepared for it. To help you, I chose two of my at bats from one game in 1985, one-on-one duels with Seattle right-handers Jim Beattie and Karl Best. I hope that by analyzing these two at bats pitch by pitch, thought by thought, you'll get a better understanding of what goes on inside my head. That should help you deal with your own confrontations, no matter what level you play on.

Friday, August 26, 1985, California vs. Seattle

Situation: Second inning. Runners on first and second, no outs. Angels have scored two runs and lead 3–1. Beattie, a 6-foot-7, 205-pound, eight-year major league veteran, is on the mound facing Gary Pettis. Count is 1-2. Carew on deck.

Carew: In this case I'm thinking that Gary should be looking to make contact and get at least one of the two runners into scoring position. That way, with a sacrifice fly or a hit we can get another run in or keep the rally going. Gary is a tough player to double up because of his speed, so almost anything on the ground will move up the runners.

Action: Pettis takes a called third strike.

Carew: Beattie threw Gary a fastball in on his hands, a tough pitch, one Gary will learn to spoil (hit foul) as he gets more experience. I credit Beattie here. He made a great pitch.

As I move into the batter's box, I'm retracing my past against this pitcher. After eight years of battles I know what his ball does, how he likes to pitch me. I realize a 3–1 lead this early in the game means nothing, but I know another base hit means one more run, some breathing room for our ball club. So I'm looking base hit all the way. I'm not looking to move the runners over at this point. Not with one out. We've got Seattle on the ropes, one good shot away from a knockout. And I want to throw a big punch.

As I step into the box, smoothing out the dirt, planting my foot, I flash on my .400 average lifetime against Beattie. I'm 0 and 1 so far tonight, but he didn't do anything different from my first time up from what he had done in previous years. "Pick up the ball," I tell myself. "Put it in play." I'm after a pitch I can drive; I'm not interested in going fishing, chasing sliders or sinkers. I know that Beattie has a tendency to get his fastball up, so I'm standing a bit more upright now, getting on a plane I feel the ball will be arriving on.

Action: Fastball in. Strike one called. 0-1.

Carew: Good pitch. He threw me a fastball that started on the inside edge and came back over the plate. It's the type of pitch I know from past experience ties me up, so this being the first pitch, I take it rather than swinging and grounding out weakly to second or short. Now, with an 0-1 count, my thinking doesn't really change. I'm still looking for my pitch. I don't feel I'm behind; I treat it just like 0-0. I'm still looking for something I can get full arm extension on, something to drive to the opposite field. I want to drive that runner on second home.

Action: Fastball inside. Ball one. 1-1.

Carew: As I picked up that pitch right out of Beattie's hand, I knew it was a pitch to take. It seems that Beattie, or his catcher, or his coaching staff has decided to pitch me with fastballs in, jamming me so I can't extend my arms. I file that away. Now, after two inside fastballs, I'm thinking outside. Yet I'm ready just in case Beattie tries to slip something past me inside.

I settle back in. Beattie sees this and steps off the rubber. So I step out, relaxing. "He's trying to get himself under control," I think to myself. So I did the same.

He's back on the rubber now, but still taking his time. I step out again. A lot of times, when a pitcher displays this much indecision, he's either confused about pitch selection or trying to break your timing and concentration. You can't let that happen. That's why I stepped out. I'm letting Beattie know *I'm* in control of this confrontation. I'm making him wait for me, to pitch to me on my terms, on my schedule. It's easier to step out and start the process all over again than it is to try to set any endurance records.

I step back in. More trouble. Beattie's veteran catcher, Bob Kearney, calls a time-out. Now I know something's up. It's possible that they can't decide what pitch to throw, but more important, I think Kearney senses Beattie's struggling. I know from checking out Beattie's statistics that he finishes only about one of every six games he starts; he knows the game is on the verge of getting out of hand. This next pitch has to be his pitch; he knows he can't make a mistake. This puts me at a decided advantage because this pitch is more important to him than to me. He doesn't want to get behind in the count, and I'm perfectly comfortable hitting with two strikes, especially in a game where we're already two runs up.

Action: Sinker away. Ball two. 2-1.

Carew: A tempting offer, but I'm not in the mood to go fishing. I see the movement of the ball early and quickly decide it's nothing I'd be interested in. I thought he might go outside and he did, but it cost him because he missed, if only by a couple of inches. Now I'm up 2-1 and in the driver's seat. In this situation you want to be very selective. This is one of the best possible counts for any hitter (2-0 being the best). Now, if you get the pitch or location you want, let 'er rip. You can always pass on a pitch that ties you up or surprises you.

In this case, be very selective of the pitches you'll swing at. If they're not in the very precise area you want them to be in, "spit on it," as we say in the majors: take a look and let it pass. There's plenty more to come.

Action: Fastball. Up, a little out, but over the plate.
Carew: This is the pitch Beattie has thrown me for years. It's also one of the reasons I'm hitting .400-plus lifetime against him. It's a pitch I've taken to left field hundreds of times in my career, and this time it's no different. As soon as he releases the ball, I know it's my pitch all the way. I remain patient—waiting, striding, wrists cocked—then explode at the pitch as it reaches the outside edge of the contact zone. Releasing my hands, I see the ball traveling to left-center; I've hit it well, it's slicing away from the center fielder, Phil Bradley, who has been playing me a little shallow. I know it's a double all the way. Standing on second base, I feel that familiar inner glow come over me. I've done my job. I knocked in a run, kept the rally going. I feel even better when the next hitter, Juan Beniquez, hits a three-run homer to put us ahead 7–1.

Situation: Same game, fifth inning, no outs, runners at first and second, reliever Karl Best (6-foot-4, 215) now pitching. This is his first full season in the league. Score still 7–1 Angels.

Carew: In the on-deck circle I'm thinking once again that Gary has to get the runners over. We're in position to put this game totally out of sight, but Gary has to do his job.

Action: Pettis grounds to the right side, advancing the runners to second and third.
Carew: Nice job, Gary. A base hit here and this game is over. I haven't hit against Best too much, a couple of times in spring training and earlier, in the third inning, when he walked me on a 3-1 count. I know from past experience he's very strong and has trouble throwing his breaking ball for strikes, so he throws mostly fastballs—the prototypical short reliever, a carbon copy of Beattie. I won't alter my batting stance too much.

But, to be honest, I'm not expecting Seattle to pitch to me. First base is open, there's one out, and Beniquez, a right-hander, is on deck. Best looks like he can be tough on righties, and Juan doesn't have the best running speed, so the situation is ripe for a double play if they put me on intentionally.

I step into the box, again making sure I'm set. Looking up, I notice the infield is drawn in. And Kearney's giving a sign. They're going to pitch to me—with the infield in, no less! Somebody hasn't done his homework. In 1984 I got the runner home from third base with less than two outs almost 80 percent of the time (11 out of 14 attempts). Now, to make matters worse (for them), they've brought the infield in, making me a .500 hitter. All I have to do is hit the ball hard on the ground, especially on artificial turf, and it's going to be a run. I can't believe they're pitching to me. Oh, well, their mistake. Best winds, delivers . . .

Action: Fastball, high and tight. Ball one.
Carew: He brushed me back. I'm not happy and shoot Best a stare. You're either going to pitch to me or walk me, but don't go throwing the ball under my chin. Go with your best stuff. Don't play with me in this situation. The stare says, "You can't intimidate me, pal." Now I'm even more determined to get him. I have at times hit

a ball hard and right back at a pitcher when I've been unnecessarily thrown at, but this is not the time for it. I can hurt him more by making sure I get the runs home. I make a minor adjustment in my stance, coiling a little to make sure I keep my front shoulder in.

Action: Slider inside, fouled off to the left side. Count is 1-1.
Carew: Pretty good pitch by Best, hard slider that jammed me inside. I opened up a bit too quickly, pulling off the ball and fouling it away. I was trying to go to the opposite field and knew I didn't have the right mechanics on the swing, but my hand action allowed me to keep the ball in foul territory. Now I'm thinking I need to look for a pitch that I can take a better cut at. I'm also aware that Best has made his first two pitches inside to me, as Beattie did in the second.

Catchers fall into patterns too. After two pitches in the second inning, Beattie went outside. The chances are good that Kearney will call for an outside pitch, but again I'll stay flexible enough in my thinking and mechanics to handle an inside pitch if one is offered.

Action: Fastball in.
Carew: As soon as I see the ball, I know it's a pitch to hit. The seams are spinning back toward the pitcher: I know it's a fastball and that it's going to be inside. It's a pitch I can drive into left or right, but instead of turning on the pitch, running the risk of grounding out to second, I keep my hands back and, at the last moment, let them explode into the ball, making sweet, solid contact to left-center.

Bradley is still playing shallow and, again, I know this is a two-base hit. The ball takes one hop and goes into the stands for a ground-rule double. We're ahead 9–1 now, and this game is over. I've knocked in three runs, scored a fourth, and feel pretty good. But I'm not quite done. Now on second base, I still have some unfinished business. I stare at Best until he sees me. After that brushback I wanted to make sure he me standing on second, that he knew I was there because he didn't do his job. A subtle psych job, but effective nonetheless. Can't let these kids get too cocky.

After the game, I review in my mind every pitch and every situation of that night's play. One thing is consistently clear: Seattle is going to try to attack me inside this year. It's a pattern that did hold up throughout the remainder of the year and, thanks in part to the input gained in this game, I went on to have a very good 1985 against the Mariners.

Chapter 6

Situational Hitting

How do you become a top situational hitter? By etching two words into your mind: confidence and selection.

Baseball is nothing if not a game of situations. Bunt, bunt-and-run, hit-and-run, sacrifice fly, pinch-hitting, designated hitting. They all combine to make baseball a game within a game, a chess match played out in cleats. Players are often remembered (or forgotten) for their ability (or inability) to produce in situational baseball. Did he move the runner over when necessary? Could he hit the sacrifice fly? Was he a clutch player off the bench? Could he be counted on to deliver a big single when it mattered? All of these attributes go into being called a "team" or "clutch" player, revered words in any sport. But such respect from your peers doesn't come easily. You have to earn it and prove it on the field, every day, day in and day out.

How do you become a top situational hitter? By etching two words into your mind: confidence and selection. You have to *believe* you can move a runner over or deliver the key sacrifice fly. You need supreme confidence, something I believe stems from study, observation, and conversation with players and coaches. It's the only way to learn what pitches to expect in certain situations. You must also develop a keen awareness of the count, what pitches you can expect at 2-1, 2-0, 1-2. Then you must learn to be ready mentally; preparation can, and often does, make the difference between a ground ball to second with a runner on third and a sacrifice fly to the outfield that scores a run.

One of the problems associated with situational hitting is, quite frankly, that some hitters don't enjoy the situations, the pressure

Communication is an important key in successful situational hitting. Rely on your manager or coach to make sure you understand your task in each situation. If you aren't sure of the signal you have been given, call time-out and ask.

or the thought of giving up an at bat. Players today, with their incentive-filled contracts and bonuses, have become very stat-minded, very individualistic in their approach to the game. All many think of is, "Well, it's a sure out and my average is going to drop." Nice attitude. What they're really thinking is, "Sure, I can move the guy over, but maybe I can get a base hit, score the run, and be the hero," or "I'll go to the right side, but I'm not grounding out. I'm driving that ball between first and second," or "I can hit a homer off this guy; I'm taking the first good pitch downtown." (The last two comments are usually followed up by a pop-up to the infield or a strikeout.)

It's hard to believe, but many major league ballplayers are oblivious of game situations, how the game evolves and the chess match between managers, particularly in late innings. They haven't been schooled enough to think ahead, to organize their

A hitter should never be fooled on a 2-0 count. On a 2-0 or 3-1 pitch you are looking for a particular pitch in an exact zone that you can drive. Your hitting zone gets reduced in size. On a 3-0 count, if you get the green light, that zone should be even smaller. These are "hitters' counts."

attack. Consequently, when called upon they quickly appear lost, for safety's sake reverting back to the ever-popular "get a hit" mentality—a strategy that brings pleasure to any pitcher's heart, a strategy I suggest has no place in this or any other sport.

Therefore, when you step up to the plate in a given situation, you have to be totally aware, tuned in to your job. If that means making an out to help the team win, so be it. No player's batting average is more important than the team's winning percentage. Your mind must be focused: get the job done. That was one of the greatest things about Frank Robinson—a former American League and National League MVP—as a hitter. Some of his prettiest swings came while moving a hitter over from first to second.

In situational hitting, a single, universal premise applies: look for *the* pitch that will allow you to accomplish the task at hand. Wait until you get that pitch, at least until you have two strikes.

Finally, before discussing specific situations, I want to reiterate one point made in Chapter 4. Unless a situation dictates otherwise, as a hitter you're concentrating on "up the middle/opposite field," adjusting your stroke to the location of the pitch. In short, staying within yourself, fighting the tendency to pull every pitch.

Hitting in Specific Counts

You'll need to know how to handle a variety of situations, so here goes. The count is:

0-1. An 0-1 count is almost the same as an 0-0 account, and your approach should be pretty much the same. You're not too far behind in the count and should still be looking for *your* pitch, something you can get full arm extension on and drive for a base hit.

0-2. This time you have to forget about location, pitch, everything. Just find the ball as quickly as possible and attack it, letting your reflexes take over. In many cases it can be easier to hit when behind 0-2 than at 0-1 because your concentration level naturally rises. The secret is not to get rattled and start guessing or fishing for anything. To do this, wait as long as possible before committing.

2-1. You're in the driver's seat with a 2-1 account. Other than 2-0, this is probably the best count a hitter can find himself in. You can be selective here, but take an aggressive cut if you see something you like. Otherwise, take the pitch and wait for the next one.

3-0. An automatic take unless the hit sign is flashed by your coach or manager. Don't try to be a hero. Play by the rules. If you get the take sign, take the pitch. Don't be messing around, dropping your body or bat into the strike zone. If you do get the green light, however, use some discipline. Most times the power hitters will be given the hit-away sign, simply because with one swing they can produce big results. But if you do get the go-ahead, power or not, don't swing at any old fastball. You have to be sure it's in your power zone. You're too far ahead in the count to hit anything but a prime pitch. And don't be foolish and try to put one out of the park. Just take your regular cut, focusing in on the target spot. This way you'll get a full and aggressive swing.

3-1. Another great time for selective hitting. Don't chase. Have confidence that you can make solid contact with two strikes. Your own strike zone remains much the same as 3-0, eyeing a pitch either down the middle or to your strengths.

3-2. No real edge here. Can't just look fastball, not these days, so watch for the baseball. Think release point. Hit the ball where it's pitched. Don't look location. Just look for the baseball and adjust accordingly.

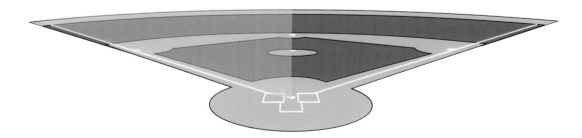

As a lefty, this was my primary target area when hitting away: up the middle or to the opposite field.

Situation 1: Advancing the Base Runner

One of the most common—but bedeviling—situations in the game is advancing a base runner. The object seems simple: hit the ball on the ground to the right side, moving the runner into scoring position. It becomes even more important when moving a runner from second to third, where he can score on a wild pitch, error, ground out, sacrifice fly, or base hit. The biggest variable in this situation is whether you hit right- or left-handed. For my money—and perhaps I'm showing my left-handed prejudice here—it's much easier for a righty to handle this advance. Two reasons: it's easier for a righty to "inside-out" a pitch to the right side, and if a righty wants to bunt the man over, he can use a push bunt to the second or first baseman. (I would guard against trying to drop a bunt down the third-base line. Unless it's perfect, the pitcher or catcher will cover it, either holding the runner at second or throwing him out at third. Only a bunt that forces the third baseman to field the ball far enough up the line to prevent him from reaching back and tagging the runner will work.)

To move a man over or to successfully hit and run you must put the ball in play and hit it on the ground behind the runner. Here the hitter has found a pitch that he can hit down and through on. He's hit the ball to the right side of the field and done his job.

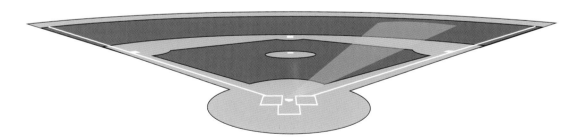

Target Zone: Moving a runner from first to second.

For the left-handed hitter, getting the runner over requires a bit more planning, a finer touch. The pitcher, wary of you pulling a pitch, is more than likely working you away. To pull a pitch in the middle of the plate means increasing the influence of the top hand during the swing. I don't mean rolling your wrists, just forcing your top hand through quicker to get the bat head out in front of the plate. Your hands should still be flat on contact, but the barrel end of the bat will be closer to the pitcher.

You should also consider the count. With no strikes or one strike, if the pitch is not one you can pull, take it, even if it's a strike. Or, better yet, you might try this trick: Move closer to home plate, crowding the inside corner. Maybe the catcher will notice this and, for the sake of a quick out, signal for a heater inside. His thinking might be that the pitcher can jam you, get the weak pop-up or ground ball. But since you set this scam up, you know what he's thinking; you're prepared for the hard stuff inside. So you release your hands a little earlier. You think bat speed and bat head. And you pull that pitch on the ground to second, easily advancing the runner. With two strikes, a good pitcher has greater leverage, much more control over the situation, so you can't be worried about a shifting defense or hitting a ball into a specific area (unless, of course, a manager insists you try, despite the count). Instead, you should concentrate on contact and putting the ball in play. Don't overswing. As time and your baseball skills improve, you can begin to think contact and advancement.

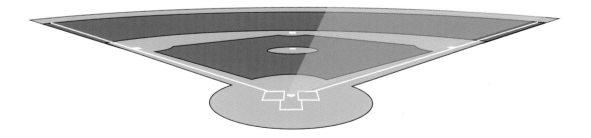

Target Zone: Moving a runner from second to third.

Situation 2: Runner Stealing Second

Let me give you an example of how we handled this situation with the Angels. Gary Pettis had tremendous speed and was an accomplished base stealer. Nine times out of ten, when Gary was on base, much like a José Reyes or a Michael Bourn today, he was thinking, "I'm going." In that case, if there were no outs or one out, and I was batting behind Gary, I took a strike. I was willing to reduce my strike allotment by one third so that Gary had a chance to move into scoring position. If the runner doesn't go and you took a strike, then you simply resume normal hitting. You should not consider taking a strike as a disadvantage. As you help the runner, he is helping you. You benefit because he's causing the pitcher to split his attention and not concentrate fully on getting you out. He's also helping you because you'll see more fastballs from a pitcher trying to reduce the runner's chances of stealing second. But if you let him steal and he's successful, now you've opened the game up and changed the situation. Now the situation looks like this: less than two outs and a runner on second. Now you can move the man over with a bunt or ground ball to the opposite side, setting up a sacrifice-fly situation. See how the simple matter of taking one strike in the right spot can, in the end, mean the difference between scoring and not scoring?

Okay, in this situation, when it's necessary, what's the easiest way to tell the runner you're taking a pitch? There's really a couple of ways. You can talk about the situation before the game or the at bat, letting him know you're taking a strike every time he's on base with less than two outs. You can also set up some silent code between you, a tip of the cap, a tap of the bat on your right shoe, anything simple—and visible—that tells your teammate you're taking. That way you'll avoid embarrassing and frustrating situations such as this: 2-0 count, runner stealing without your knowledge, and you rip a line drive that is easily turned into a double play.

Important: If the runner isn't as quick—say a David Ortiz instead of a Jacoby Ellsbury—I'd give away a strike only if so instructed by the third-base coach or manager.

Sometimes, in the case of a slower runner who is ordered to steal, you can help him out. The best way to help out is to block the catcher's view, to disrupt the catcher's timing. Or just drop your bat into the strike zone (don't keep it there too long or the umpire may call a swinging strike). Pull it out as the pitch approaches. Also, you could bend over the plate a bit—nothing drastic, just enough to disrupt the catcher's timing and release. That extra millisecond or two it takes for the catcher to move around you might make the difference between a safe or out call at second.

Situation 3: Hit-and-Run

Runner on first, less than two outs. Runner stealing. You're expected to protect him, ideally getting a base hit into the area vacated by the infielder who covers second base. The cardinal rule here is *hit the ball anywhere on the ground*. You don't want fly balls. You don't want line drives. Your job is to hit a ground ball. Where you hit this ball obviously depends on the pitch. Normally, the shortstop will cover for left-handed hitters, the second baseman for right-handed hitters. For me it was a bit different, thanks to my reputation as an opposite-field hitter (the shortstop normally stayed put, eliminating my favorite hole). But no matter who covers, don't try to adjust *during* the pitch. If the second baseman is covering and it's a fastball outside, don't try at the last second to hit the ball into the hole at second. It won't work. If the ball is away, get it in play someplace, any place. You have to put it in play. Just think, "Hit the ball on the ground."

Do you have to swing at every pitch when the hit-and-run is called? You do if your manager says so. But sometimes, if there's good speed at first and the pitch is in the dirt, you might want to hold up, not wasting a swinging strike. Of course, with Larry Leadfoot on the move, you've got to protect him no matter where the ball is pitched, even if you foul the ball off. Finally, don't try to overpower the pitch. Think contact and try not to uppercut.

When to Use the Hit-and-Run

Here is a bit of baseball strategy mixed in with the situations. Of course, whether your team plays the speed game or relies on the long ball depends on your players. For much of their storied history, the Boston Red Sox had little use for the hit-and-run over the years. The strategy for a team built for the quaint confines of Fenway Park was power over speed, though the team's makeup has changed to include power and speed over the years. Still, playing the power game in Fenway or the new Yankee Stadium or Houston's Minute Maid Park generates more runs than it would, say, at the Mets' Citi Field. In a power-friendly ballpark, you don't want to give up outs at second base when you have four or five potential 20-home-run hitters in the lineup. On other teams, however, like the Mets, the "rabbits" set the table for guys like David Wright and Carlos Beltrán. You let guys like the Yankees' Brett Gardner or José Reyes or Jacoby Ellsbury run because you've got excellent contact hitters like Derek Jeter or Wright or Adrian Gonzalez hitting behind them. Most of the better hitters can handle the bat well enough to take a strike, let the man steal, then move him over to third with a ground ball. But if you've got a slow runner on first, I say forget the steal and go with the hit-and-run. It's a play that I loved, yet see less and less of each year.

Whether you're facing a righty or a lefty, it's your job to hang in there and stay aggressive. Maintain that mental edge no matter what the situation.

Situation 4: Lefty vs. Lefty and Righty vs. Righty

One of the things that bothers me most these days is the notion that lefties can't hit lefties and righties can't hit righties. Managers have taken an advantage (or possible advantage) situation and applied a universal application. Yes, a left-handed pitcher has a slight advantage over a left-handed hitter because his curveball breaks away. But I have to tell you, I didn't get 3,053 hits batting exclusively against right-handed pitchers. Good hitters hit all pitching. For some reason, with more coaches going to a platoon system, kids are starting to believe they can't hit left-handers if they're left-handed themselves. Don't believe it. A righty with a .300 average has a better chance of getting a hit off a right-handed pitcher than a lefty with a .250 average.

What happens when you face a pitcher coming from the same side as you is a tendency to bail out or pull off the ball. Knowing this, you must discipline yourself to stay in there, to keep your head on the ball, to force yourself to be aggressive mentally. Drill it in: don't give an inch. And if you make an out, it's not because you're both right-handed or both left-handed. It's because pitchers get .300 hitters out 7 out of 10 times.

Situation 5: Relief Pitching

A word to the wise: don't let it shake you up. So they throw hard. Big deal. If you know who the pitcher is, what's up his sleeve, you can compete. You have some advantages, too. When a reliever comes in, especially to snuff out a threat, his job is to throw strikes. You know the ball is going to be around the plate. And with certain guys—like Jordan Walden with the Angels, the Dodgers' Jonathan Broxton, and Kyle Farnsworth of the Tampa Bay Rays—90 percent of the time it's going to be the fastball. Nothing fancy. Just some heavy heat, but if you're geared for it, you're on even terms.

Of course, at the high-school level or below, relief pitching isn't so predictable. Sure, they *want* to throw strikes, but can they? Here you want to be a bit more cautious. Don't expect anything; just work the count as you would with any other pitcher (advantage to you on 2-0 or 3-1; to the pitcher on 0-1 or 0-2). Anticipate hard stuff when he's behind in the count, off-speed stuff when you're in a hole, but don't commit to it ahead of time. It's a good idea in high school to keep a notebook on the pitchers you face, just as many major-leaguers do. That way, come tournament time or during league play or even in the playoffs, you can look up 'ol No.27 and see what he was throwing three weeks earlier.

Situation 6: Hitting with the Infield In

The easiest way to hit .500 is when the infield is playing you in. Playing in, the infielders have a drastically reduced range. They have little chance of making a play on the ball unless it is hit directly at them. Still, for some unknown reason, hitters feel compelled to try to hit the ball over or through people. Forget it. The hitter needs to concentrate on getting a good pitch and driving it to the big part of the field.

Situation 7: Being a Hero

World Series time. Bottom of the ninth, bases loaded, two outs. Score tied or one run down. Think fast now. Would you want to be in that situation? I would. You know why? Because anytime I can get a base hit to win a ballgame, I want to. I can go back

Everyone dreams of being a hero and helping their team win the big game. If you put preparation and dedication ahead of that dream, no situation will be too big for you.

to 1982 and vividly recall the last out of the season for the California Angels. I made it. We were in the American League Championship Series, and Brian Downing was at the plate with Ron Jackson on second representing the tying run. I remember telling myself, "C'mon, Brian, give me a shot!" At that moment, I felt I was going to get the base hit to tie the game for us. I got my chance, went to the plate feeling more confident than ever, and I hit a bullet—unfortunately it was right into the glove of Brewers shortstop Robin Yount.

But that's life. I always wanted to win a game for my club. So should you. Why put it on someone else's shoulders? You're prepared. You've studied the pitcher. This is what the game is all about. If you fail, fine; you did your best. But take a deep breath, step into the box, and accept the challenge.

Situation 8: Pinch-Hitting

There are two kinds of pinch hitters. One group specializes in pinch-hitting, guys over the years like Rusty Staub, Lenny Harris, and Matt Stairs. That's their job. That's why they played or are still playing in the big leagues. The other, much more common group consists of non-regulars and veterans too old to play every day. No matter what the category, one premise prevails: *you have to realize your role on the club is going to be judged, at least in part, on how you perform in the pinch.* So take it seriously. You must learn to control the mental drudgery, the frustrations, not getting too high or too low. Work to be prepared. How do you do that? By taking extra pre-game hitting. By using the hours of extra time you have in the dugout to your best advantage. By concentrating on getting a good swing on every pitch. By knowing what you want to accomplish and how to accomplish it.

In my mind, when you leave the bench to pinch-hit, you're not going up there to take a strike (unless the situation specifically dictates it). You're up there to get on base or win a game. So swing the bat. A lot of well-prepared pinch hitters will jump on the first good pitch they see, simply because they know they're not going to see too many good pitches if they get behind in the count. Of course, on occasion that strategy will backfire, as it did even to a hitter as good as Hal McRae in a crucial World Series situation against John Tudor of the Cardinals in 1985. McRae, who was normally the designated hitter for Kansas City before later becoming the franchise's manager, had been relegated to the bench by the rule then calling for the DH to be used in the series only in even-numbered years. McRae was called to pinch-hit in the seventh inning of the fourth game of the series with the bases loaded and his team trailing 3–0. Now, McRae was a notorious first-ball hitter. Tudor knew that. So instead of feeding him a fastball to get ahead in the count (McRae probably would have taken a terrific cut at it), Tudor nibbled on the outside corner with a sinker. The overanxious McRae took the bait, tapping a harmless ground ball to third. So much for the threat.

The moral here, obviously, is not to fall into a pattern as a pinch hitter. Sure, be ready for the heater; you're going to see it 80 percent of the time in this situation, particularly in close games with runners on base. But, by the same token, have confidence in your ability to hit with two strikes. Build that confidence by working on just that situation during batting practice. Pretend the count is 1-2, 2-2, or 3-2. You have to swing on the next pitch. Do that over and over each day. When you finally get into that situation during a game, you'll have the confidence to know you can deliver.

Like any other hitting situation, the sacrifice fly calls for the hitter to be selective and recognize a pitch he can drive in the air. Here the hitter has found a pitch on which he can get good extension, and he gets the runner home.

It's also important to stay in the game, even when you're on the bench. Don't look into the stands or spend time making idle chatter. Of course, it helps if the manager tells you an inning or two beforehand to get ready, but, honestly, some managers are too busy. So it's up to you. You have to follow the game from the first out, thinking ahead to situations. Who's been pitching middle relief for this team? What pitches do they use when they're ahead? These are all questions one asks before a game anyway, but they become doubly important in a pinch-hitting situation. You have only one shot at hitting—not three or four—so prepare yourself to make the best of it.

Pinch-hitting isn't just a mental game. You should stretch out vigorously before a game, then plan to work your arms and legs between innings. When the call comes, you're not going to have five minutes to get loose. You might get 60 seconds for a couple of knee bends and trunk twisters. You have to be ready. That means swinging a weighted bat between innings, in the clubhouse or behind the bench if you can. As you swing, concentrate on fundamentals: head down, quick bat, weight transfer, keeping the front shoulder in.

Also, if you're not starting because of a manager's decision or a personal slump, don't sulk. You never know what might happen. If a teammate gets hurt or ejected, you might be in as early as the first inning. If you're not loose or involved in the game, you're nothing but an automatic out. That's one of the things I respected most about my California Angels manager, Gene Mauch. If I wasn't playing, he'd tell me up-front, warning me, "If the game gets close or they change pitchers, I want you ready." That's all a ballplayer can ask of his manager. You can't expect them to babysit you.

Situation 9: Designated Hitting

Designated hitting has been a thorny issue since its introduction in the American League in 1973. The purists object to its use, bemoaning lost strategy. "Reformists" insist it adds runs—and excitement—to the game. Pro or con, it's tough to DH. You're basically being asked to pinch-hit four or five times in a game. The mental strain is rough; you hit and return right to the bench, unable to erase mistakes or frustrations with some fancy fielding. Again, the key here is preparation. Go to the clubhouse or behind the bench and swing a bat, hit a ball off a batting tee, or get someone to soft-toss you pitches you can hit into a net. Do whatever you can to stay loose. Jog easily behind the bench. Stay mentally sharp. One big difference between a good DH and a mediocre one is in their mental approach. You have to steel yourself to the situation, accepting, for the moment, that you're a hitter and nothing more. And if you make an out, accept it. Yes, you should analyze why (bad swing, bad pitch, and so on), but don't dwell on the past—bad or good. You can't labor over any at bat. If you do, the mental strain will wear you down and you'll end up playing full-time again, but it will be in the minor leagues.

Situation 10: Bad Weather

When the Twins opened the beautiful new Target Field in 2010, much speculation centered on outdoor baseball and the effects the cold weather would have on hitters early in the season. Truth is, cold weather benefits the hitter because you will see more fastballs from pitchers who can't get a good grip on their breaking pitches. Ultimately, a hitter needs to focus on the game and get the job done—whether it's 100 degrees or 35.

No one likes to play in the cold or rain, but you still have a job to do. Regardless of what the weather man throws your way, buckle down and focus on baseball. *Shutterstock*

Chapter 7 Bunting

Bunting has become a lost art in the game of baseball. Players today are so caught up in hitting the ball into the seats, even in batting practice, they forget—or, worse, don't care enough—to hone their other skills. The result: when the time comes for them to sacrifice a runner over or squeeze him home or beat out a drag bunt to start a rally, they fail miserably, disgracing themselves, often contributing to a team defeat. One of the best bunters of the past 50 years was also a great power hitter: Mickey Mantle. Mantle was very smart and, before injury took its toll on his legs, a very speedy player. He knew full well the wisdom of a good bunt and he valued the bunt for more than the occasional base hit or, if the situation called for it, the means by which to move a base runner over. Those are obvious. Often overlooked is how the bunt causes the third baseman to cheat in at the corner, thereby decreasing his range and reaction time to a ball hit in his direction.

Late in my career, I read that I didn't bunt for base hits as much as I did earlier in my career. It was true. In my early days, I'd pick up 20 to 30 hits a year on bunts. One year I was 28 for 34. But as my playing days came to an end, I didn't run as well as I had in my younger days and, perhaps more importantly, third basemen around the league had gotten wise to me. But, with them playing in, I picked up 15 to 20 hits a year by slapping the ball past them. So, though I didn't bunt for as many hits as I once had, I could directly attribute a similar number of base hits to the threat of a bunt. Over the course of my career, I bunted .795, with 151 hits in 190 attempts.

In recent years, former National League Rookie of the Year runner-up Willy Taveras was one of baseball's best bunters. A career .274 hitter, 108 of his 558 hits came on bunts. In 2007 alone he bunted .750 (27 for 36).

The Sacrifice Bunt

The first thing a hitter must understand when he's in a sacrifice situation is that he has one job at the plate and one job only: to advance the runner. The term "sacrifice" means just that: "giving up" your at bat for the good of the team. Forget about bunting for a base hit; get the ball on the ground and advance the runner over. Think "we" instead of "I."

To be successful, remember that bunting is no different from any other form of situational hitting. The basics remain the same.

We bunt either for a base hit or to advance a runner. The single most important rule in successful bunting is that the barrel of the bat *must* be higher than the handle of the bat when the bat contacts the ball. If you keep this in mind, you will also be less likely to bunt at bad pitches.

You must look for a pitch that you can handle. In a bunt situation, that means a pitch in the middle third of the strike zone. One of the keys to being a good bunter is the angle of your bat upon contact with the ball. You have to keep the barrel end of the bat slightly higher than the handle. If you drop the barrel, the bat head has an overwhelming tendency to angle toward foul territory and the ball either strikes the top half of the bat (popping up) or is steered foul, neither of which suits your purpose. On a lower pitch, use your legs to get down to the ball, not your bat.

What about the sacrifice bunt? The conventional way of teaching it is for the hitter to square around—something I never felt comfortable with. Instead, I favored only a slight pivot of my feet and upper body, which minimized movement of my head and body. This bunting alignment is also more comfortable, as my position in the batter's box was similar to my normal hitting stance. More important, I could see the ball better. As a hitter, you are accustomed to seeing the pitch in a certain way. If you're a lefty, your right eye is closer to the pitcher; the opposite holds if you're

Each of these photos illustrates what happens when the barrel of the bat gets below the handle of the bat: You foul the ball off, doing your team no good at all.

right-handed. When a batter squares all the way around and both eyes face the pitcher, he sees the pitch from a different perspective as it approaches the plate. With my pivot system, your head is in the same position for the bunt as when you hit normally; therefore, you're going to see the ball approach the plate in the same way you see every other pitch. That's obviously to your advantage.

Now, let's get a little more technical. When I walked into the batter's box to sacrifice bunt, nothing changed from my regular stance: I set up in the exact same position in the batter's box; I gripped my bat with the same loose and comfortable grip; I prepared to hit as if I was going to take a full swing. As the pitcher came set, I made my move, pivoting on my toes, my heels moving clockwise about 3 inches. This forced my lower body around so that my belt buckle was facing toward the shortstop (second baseman if you're right-handed). My head and upper body had not moved. My knees were slightly bent, and my weight was on the balls of my feet. If the catcher doesn't notice, you may be able to move up subtly in the batter's box. This can help you get your bat into fair territory.

As you make the pivot, the top hand slides up the bat about 3 to 3 1/2 inches. The bottom hand becomes the anchor of the bat, the top hand the rudder. You want those hands to be soft on the bunt. You don't want to "choke" your bat with a death grip, because a tight trip will cause the ball to jump off your bat upon contact. A soft grip deadens the ball, allowing me to "catch" it on the bat.

Now, you've made your pivot and have your hands in position on the bat. Step three occurs as the ball is in flight. I would make a circular motion clockwise with the barrel end of the bat. Remember we talked about how important it is to keep the barrel of the bat higher than the handle? In watching hitters, I've noticed that when they square around, they immediately put their bats into the bunting position. What happens is that as they watch the pitch, the fat end of the bat has a tendency to drop during the anticipatory period, causing foul balls. This concept, "catching the ball" on the bat, was a major factor in my success as a bunter.

As in hitting, the key to good bunting is soft hands. Notice in this sequence how I cradle the bat. I want my bottom hand to manipulate the handle, and I want as little pressure on my top hand as possible so the barrel of the bat can absorb and deaden the ball's movement on impact. Don't "jab" the ball; let it come to you and catch it, with the bat giving slightly on contact.

As you can see, there's a lot going on, and we've yet to make contact. The last step prior to contact is to move the bat from twelve o'clock into the two o'clock position. The key to making good contact as a bunter is the exact opposite of what we teach for making good contact as a hitter. In hitting, the action we initiate thrusts the head of the bat toward the ball. In bunting, we want to let the ball come toward the bat. A big mistake bad bunters make is trying to jab the bat toward the ball. Once you've moved your bat into the bunting zone, the only time that bat, or any part of your body, should move is when the ball actually makes contact with the bat. I like to call it catching the ball with your bat. That's really what bunting is.

Okay, let's try it. Place your bat into the anticipated line of flight of the ball. Your hands should hold the bat softly, so softly that at impact the bat gives lightly as the ball drops to the ground. Picture the bat "catching" the ball, being the fielder, not the hitter.

All right, let's review some keys to successful sacrifice bunting:

- Go up to the plate intent on making an out to help your team.

- Look for a pitch in the upper half of the strike zone to bunt.

- Pivot your lower body while keeping your head and upper body still, so you can see the ball hit the bat.

- Keep the barrel end of the bat higher than the handle end.

- Grip the bat as loosely as possible.

- Let the ball come to you and "catch" it with your bat.

With all that in mind, I must confess it's the way I *teach* the sacrifice bunt. It's not exactly the way I *did* it. There is only one difference between what I teach and what I did, and it's a worthwhile pointer for advanced bunters. As I grew more comfortable bunting, I no longer slid my hands up the handle of

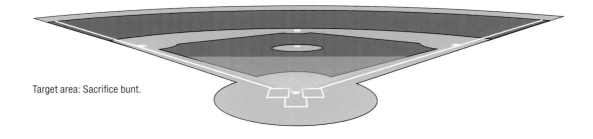

Target area: Sacrifice bunt.

the bat prior to bunting. The reason I like novice bunters (this can include big-leaguers) to slide their hands up the bat is that it gives them less bat to control. As a good bunter, I advanced to the point where the bat felt like an extension of my hand. I liked to have more bat to work with, so I did everything I teach except that I kept my hands together at the end of the bat. Either way is correct. But it's best to master the novice method before attempting a technique requiring a more delicate touch.

Bunting for a Base Hit

First of all, let's dismiss the myth that it's harder for a right-handed hitter to bunt for a base hit than it is for a left-handed hitter. Granted, a lefty is one step closer to first base, but three of the all-time best bunters—Phil Rizzuto, Mantle, and Steve Garvey—achieved great success bunting from the right side.

In bunting for a base hit, I prefer the "crossover" method, so called because as the pitch approaches, the back leg steps, or crosses, over the front leg as it moves toward the pitcher to become, in effect, your first step toward first base. At the same time, your bat should move out in front of the plate. Note that I said the crossover step is *toward the pitcher.* That way, you'll be in optimum position to bunt an outside pitch down the third-base line or an inside pitch down the first-base line. If your crossover step takes your momentum toward first base, you won't be able to bunt the outside strike.

There are two other big differences between bunting for a base hit and for the sacrifice. One is the element of surprise. More bunted base hits can be attributed to the surprise factor than to great execution. Here, right-handed hitters have an advantage over left-handed hitters, if only because infielders don't normally expect right-handed hitters to bunt. They play deeper at the corners.

You can work the surprise factor to your advantage, and I'll show you how. Needless to say, the "foul ball on a third strike and you're out" rule intimidates most players and coaches. But not Mantle, not Garvey. And even with my reputation as a bunter, I went 12 for 12 one year on two-strike bunts. Many of those hits turned into runs that helped us win ballgames. And think what a difference 12 for 12 made to my batting average.

On a sacrifice bunt, you give yourself away sooner. Everyone in the ballpark knows you're going to bunt, so just take your time, get set, then execute, placing the ball on the ground in a position where anyone but the catcher has to make the play. This is difficult, though, when you're bunting for a base hit. Then you want to delay your mechanics as long as possible, not making your initial move until just before the pitcher releases the ball. This

Often the biggest mistake a left-handed hitter makes when he bunts for a base hit is making his first move away from the pitcher and down the first-base line. To lay down a successful drag bunt, your first move needs to be toward the pitcher, although unlike in hitting, where you stride with your front foot, in a left-handed drag bunt your first move is a crossover step with your back foot *directly* toward the pitcher. From there it's easy: just keep the barrel of the bat higher than the handle, "catch" the ball lightly on the bat, and drop it down the third-base line in that no man's land, forcing the pitcher or third baseman to make a web gem to even have a chance of getting you out at first. If you want to go to the right side of the field, your goal is to get the ball past the pitcher so the second baseman has to field it. That's almost always an automatic hit.

allows plenty of time to take a crossover step, pick up the spin and location of the ball, and get your bat into bunting position. Conversely, there's not enough time for an infielder who's playing back to field a well-placed bunt and throw you out.

Okay, delaying the crossover step and the element of surprise are two keys to a successful drag bunt. Another is the distribution of your weight and your takeoff to first base. On the sacrifice, no matter whether you're right- or left-handed, your weight will be fairly evenly distributed on the balls of your feet. Not so in base-hit bunting. If you're left-handed and crossing over (as you should be), all your weight should be on the left foot at the moment of contact. That foot, in effect, becomes your starting block toward first base.

For a right-handed hitter, all of his weight will naturally be on his left foot as he steps forward upon contact. Whereas a lefty will cross over and drop his bat into bunting position, a right-handed bunter's first move should get his legs into running position as soon as the bat goes forward. The weight on the left foot again becomes the starting block for the race toward first base. Remember, a key to bunting for a hit is no wasted motion. So drop the bat at contact. Forget about it; just open your hands and let it fall. Your energies should be concentrated on getting down the line; let someone else worry about the bat. If you're lucky, maybe the catcher will trip over it.

So, as you can tell, there are two basic differences in bunting for a base hit: (1) you delay your bunting mechanics in order to take advantage of the element of surprise, and (2) your weight is on your left foot rather than evenly distributed. Everything else is the same: You still want to look for a pitch you can handle that's up in the zone. If you're left-handed, an outside pitch or a pitch down the middle goes down third; an inside pitch goes down first (and vice versa for right-handers). The barrel of the bat is higher than the handle and motionless upon contact. Keep a soft grip on the bat. And let the ball come to the bat and "catch" it upon contact.

Positioning the Ball on the Bunt

For some players, getting a bunt in fair territory is asking a lot, but as you practice more and more and begin to build your confidence, you'll get more and more aggressive, more clinical in your attempts. Personally, I dropped most of my bunts down the third-base line, especially when bunting for a base hit. You cut it too close when you bunt down the right side. You have to bunt the ball hard enough to get it between the pitcher and the first baseman so that the second baseman has to field the ball on the run, often bare-handing it, and make a shorter, but often

A drag bunt from the right side requires a little more deception than one from the left side. Mickey Mantle and Steve Garvey loved to drag bunt from the right side with two strikes in the count. You'd better be good if you are going to try that. No crossover step here. The righty needs to show bunt as late as possible and then drop the back foot before catching the ball on the bat and charging down the line.

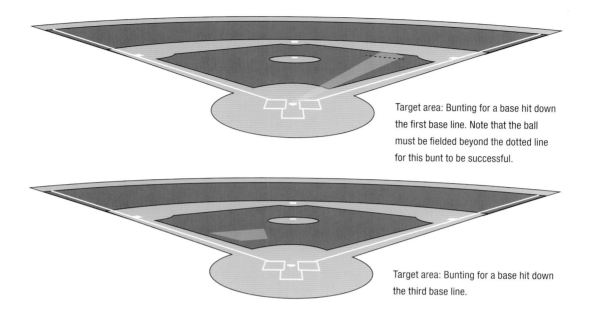

Target area: Bunting for a base hit down the first base line. Note that the ball must be fielded beyond the dotted line for this bunt to be successful.

Target area: Bunting for a base hit down the third base line.

off-balance throw. Even if the pitcher fields the ball down the third base line, a righty must stop his momentum, plant, and throw. Even better is when a lefty has to turn his body all the way around before he can make the long throw to first. So you can see why I felt my chances of bunting a base hit were 80 percent higher if I went down the third-base line instead of down first.

In a sacrifice situation, there is only one crucial role to keep in mind: bunt the ball far enough that the catcher cannot field the ball on the dirt. Preferably, don't let the catcher field the ball at all. Otherwise, on a sacrifice, just place the ball so that you don't bunt it right to a charging infielder. That means keeping your eyes open and head up—seeing who's moving in what direction. Normally, if you can make an infielder alter his charge even one step, it's enough to ensure a successful sacrifice. Another thing to keep an eye out for is the player least likely to make a good play. If you're playing Milwaukee, you're going to bunt to Prince Fielder 10 times before you'll give anybody else in the infield a chance to throw you out. But let's not get ahead of ourselves. The key to successful bunting is getting a pitch that will allow you to place the ball where you want to.

As long as we're talking about location, let's discuss bunting different pitches. Always look to bunt a fast ball. The curve changes direction and height, whereas a fastball is straight. And as we've mentioned, look for pitches that are belt high in the strike zone because we want to keep the barrel end of the bat higher than the handle. However, you also have to be prepared for the low pitch,

Notice where my back foot is on impact: it's pointing straight at the pitcher. On contact I am already in the blocks to start my sprint down the line. Early in my career I was good for about 20 hits a season from bunts. I see 10 hits in this picture alone.

because sometimes that's all that's on the menu. In that case, you must bend your knees and go down after it. Keep the barrel head up as best you can; if you have to drop too far, the pitch is more than likely a ball, so take it. But if you must alter the bat alignment to reach a low pitch, just remember to concentrate even more. You have a greater margin for error, so something has to increase—and that's your mind power.

Practice Bunting

I began this chapter by calling bunting a lost art. Where it was lost was in the batting cage, just like so many other aspects of hitting. If you want to improve, you have to pay a price. So many good younger players with great speed believe all they have to do is drop the ball down and beat it out. It doesn't happen. You have to know how, where, and when to bunt before it's going to seriously affect your average. And there's only one way to accomplish these things: through practice.

If you're just learning to bunt, don't expect miracles. Start off with 30 minutes a day, just getting the feel of the bat hitting the ball at a speed you can comfortably handle, slowly reviewing, step by step, the mechanics of the sacrifice bunt. After a while—maybe several weeks—the mechanics will become second nature to you. Gradually, as your confidence increases, so should the velocity, speed, and variety of pitches you practice bunting. Don't fret if you feel you're taking a step backward (your proficiency may drop off initially), because soon you'll be able to handle the hard stuff as well as breaking pitches. Now, once you've completed that course, go all the way back to the beginning and start over with bunting for a base hit. Thirty minutes a session, moderate speed. Practice the mechanics. Then, as you gain proficiency, speed up the pitches and start to practice bunting breaking balls.

Once you're sure you've got control over the mechanics, begin bunting into target areas. Place two or three baseballs in various spots down the third-base line, then practice bunting toward those target balls in sequence. After you've practiced hitting targets down the third-base line, go through the same drill down the first-base line. This is the same system I use to stay sharp in the offseason. (Bunting, like hitting, isn't an art you can take out of the closet any time you want and expect to be effective. It takes work all year round.) Pre-game batting practice is also a time to take your bunting seriously. Most players rush through their bunts so they can rip easy lobs over the fence. Resist that temptation. Take your time. Have a purpose; ask the BP pitcher to throw you several outside pitches while you practice bunting those balls down the appropriate line. Then have him throw you several inside pitches to bunt. Remember, bunting time during pre-game batting practice is limited, so use it wisely. Don't spend too much time bunting; three or four sacrifice and drag bunts down each line is plenty, provided you're concentrating. You can always go out early or stay late, or every so often, on a practice day, take some extra bunting practice. It's the only way I know to master the art.

The Suicide Squeeze

The suicide squeeze is one of the most exciting plays in baseball and will *always* result in a score when the batter executes his job properly. His job: get the bunt down on any given pitch. A suicide squeeze is the only time when we forget several of our disciplines. When in a suicide situation, you have to get your bat on the ball. If the pitch is low and away and you have to drop the barrel end of the bat to make contact, it's better to foul off a pitch than to have your runner picked off. If the pitch is out of the strike zone, go out and get it. Even if the ball is at your head, which is where pitchers are taught to throw in this situation, you still have to find a way to get the bat on the ball.

Chapter 8

Batting Practice and Conditioning

You must come to practice every day with a definite goal in mind.

Hitting is a subtle science, one I feel you can never learn enough about, and one in which I quickly profess to have no omnipotent powers. As my career went on, I would often react rather than think, my body and mind fused by the years I had spent whacking ball after ball in practice.

In all those years, I learned three important lessons. They were *concentration, purpose,* and *working on a weakness.* Because practice is the only place where you can experiment with suggestions and instruction, it's imperative that you develop sound work habits. Hitting .300 is a goal; it means devoting time, energy, and concentration. That's one of the biggest changes in the game today: so many of the kids coming up just don't focus on the job at hand. They see practice as social hour, a chance to show their strength or simply to fool around. They think once they've made it in the big leagues, work automatically stops. It doesn't. In fact, it can be easier to get to the big leagues than to stay there. You can't get complacent. Always take advantage of the facilities and coaches to improve your skills.

And that's where *purpose* comes in. You must come to practice every day with a definite goal in mind. You want to work on hitting curveballs. You need help on the drag bunt. In the field, you need to get rid of the ball quicker on the double play. Anything. You don't have to spend hours on your weaknesses, just as long as you recognize them as weaknesses (believe me, some scout will!) and are devoted to turning a negative into a positive. And don't blame

Coach John Wooden used to say, "Practice doesn't make perfect, perfect practice makes perfect." For me, perfect hitting practice came in 15-minute increments because I didn't want to get tired and start repeating bad swings. Here I am, hitting off the tee, working on many of the things we spoke about in Chapter 4: balance, hitting the ball out front, pivoting on my back foot. Practice with a purpose. Make every swing a perfect swing. Don't make bad swings in practice, because you don't want to lock poor habits into your muscle memory. That's a pretty good swing there, if I do say so myself.

your manager or coach for your miscues or failings. A manager doesn't bunt or move a runner over. You do. To avoid even having to *think* about making such excuses, take the importance of practice to heart. Learn that *striving* to be a great player will carry into other facets of your life—in school, in business. Planting the seeds of success at an early age can mean a big harvest later on.

As a professional, one who cared greatly about his image and batting average, I worked almost year-round. I wouldn't even have taken the four weeks off from hitting that I did in late October except that in order to get the most out of batting practice, I needed to be physically well enough to continually execute a proper swing. After 30 or so preseason games, 162 regular-season games, and playoffs (if I was lucky), the body needed a rest.

Preparing for a Season

During the offseason, I tried to hit three days a week, usually Monday, Wednesday, and Friday. After four weeks without a bat in my hands, I went back to the basics. I tried to make contact, pure and simple, performing a specific action over and over, 10 minutes a day, against easy pitching. No matter when you're taking batting practice, it's important to maintain your hitting discipline, to have a purpose for every swing. When I started hitting after a prolonged layoff, I wanted nothing but straight pitches—"easy heat" I could hit back up the middle.

After three or four weeks of this routine, I would start asking for breaking pitches, increasing my hitting time from 10 minutes to 15 minutes—never longer. Even during the season, when I was in peak condition, I wouldn't hit for longer than 15 minutes. I did this for two reasons. One is that after 15 minutes my lower back would begin to get sore. If I altered my swing to compensate for the soreness, I began to do unnatural things and pick up bad habits. It's the same when you feel tired. Second, it's difficult to maintain peak concentration and discipline beyond 15 minutes. You don't want to practice sloppy habits. I've found over the years that if you can get in 10 to 15 minutes of good, solid, disciplined hitting, you've accomplished all there is to do. Why go further? Use the time to work on other parts of your game. Run, ride an exercise bike, take ground balls. It's not a lot to ask during the offseason. Also, consider videotaping yourself to compare periods when you're a hot hitter and when you're slumping. Most important, however, is to try to get the most out of every swing. Do these things and you'll be ready to start helping your team win ballgames from opening day.

Offseason batting practice is essential to maintain your rhythm as a hitter. But don't overdo it—10–15 minutes at a time is all you need. *Shutterstock*

In-Season Practice Days

Once the season starts, you have to adapt your batting-practice schedule to your game schedule. If you're a high school or Little League player, you're playing only one or two days a week, so that leaves you three to five practice days. If you're in college or pro ball, you're playing and traveling much more often, so your challenge is to *make* the time that is necessary for quality batting practice. Quality BP is different from pre-game batting practice, which we will address later.

As discussed, never hit longer than 15 minutes on any given day, unless you're a switch hitter. Then hit 10 minutes from each side. The first few minutes, just try to get loose and make contact. You want straight pitches right down the middle; concentrate on your mechanics and think contact. As soon as you're loose, start asking the pitcher to spot the ball. Several inside, several outside, a few high and a few low. With these pitches, work on using your hands, being quick, aggressive, hitting the ball where it's pitched and using the whole field. Do this until you feel satisfied that you've achieved an acceptable level of consistency in your mechanics.

Once you've reached that level, have the batting-practice pitcher mix up his pitches and their locations so you don't know whether you'll be seeing a breaking ball or a straight pitch. This forces you to concentrate even more on reading the pitch, reacting to the ball, honing your hitting instincts and mechanics. By this time your hands are sore and you're tired, so conclude your hitting for the day.

I would, however, still bunt. We talked at length about practicing bunting in the previous chapter. But I practiced my bunting on practice days the same way I practiced hitting. Each pitch demands the utmost in discipline, the utmost in concentration. Each pitch has purpose. The same discipline I used in a game I used in bunting. Every at bat is the most important at bat of your career. And the same goes for batting practice. Approach every pitch with single-minded concentration.

While we are talking about batting practice, I'd like once again to mention bats. One of the keys to being a good hitter is knowing yourself as a hitter. Some players at lower levels can be deceived by the use of aluminum bats. Aluminum bats give hitters a false sense of their hitting capabilities. I can't tell you how many young players come to work out with us directly from high school or right out of college and can't understand why they don't hit the ball as far as they did back home. The reason is the aluminum bat. I strongly oppose using them.

Now, I'm not going to be naive enough to believe that, come game time, you're going to put aside your aluminum bat because

As I mentioned earlier, aluminum bats are the worst things to happen to hitters since the slider. It bears repeating: Even if you are going to hit with an aluminum or composite bat in a game, practice with the wooden bat so you can get a true gauge of your abilities.

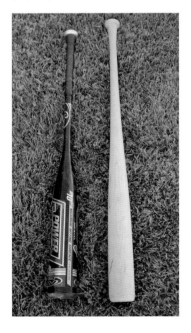

It's important to try and simulate game situations in all practice settings. If you are not going to hit with sunglasses during a game, don't wear them during batting practice. The slightest variation in your ability to track the ball on its path to home plate might be the difference between a hit and an out.

I say it's deceiving. But I am going to ask you to put it aside in the offseason and on practice days. Learn who you really are as a hitter and what your capabilities are. Then, when you hit with your aluminum bat on game day, you'll be even further ahead.

Game Days

Batting practice on game days serves several important purposes. You want to use it to get loose, to practice proper swing mechanics and lock them into your memory bank, as well as to prepare mentally for game situations and for the pitcher(s) you'll be facing that day. Too many players don't treat pre-game batting practice with the proper respect. Pre-game is the beginning of our day's work. Once I started work, I didn't want to be distracted from the task at hand. I was always willing to spend as much time as necessary with the press before my workday began. Once batting practice started, though, I was intent on preparing for the game. I had to be, because good hitting demands that kind of attention. It is an attitude that probably won't win too many friends in the media, but it will add points to your average and help your team.

On game days, be aware of your opponent's pitchers and what they throw. That's not always the easiest thing to do, but few pitchers make their debut against you. If you're going to see a curveball pitcher, ask for more breaking pitches that day. If he's a fastball pitcher, have a little more zip put on the ball. Also, in pre-game batting practice, be aware of what you need to work on. If pitchers have been jamming you lately, have your pitcher throw inside and work on moving your hands through the ball and making good contact.

Pre-game batting practice is a time for work, not for horsing around. I can't tell you how often a good session of pre-game batting practice translates into a multiple-hit game. Take that from a major-leaguer who has nearly 1,000 multiple-hit games to his credit.

There is no substitution for hitting live pitching. Hopefully you will always get cuts against live pitching on game days. If so, try to get a few swings against both right- and left-handed pitchers whenever possible.

Two other points about pre-game batting practice. Whenever possible, try to take a round or two against a right-hander *and* against a left-hander, because even though a righty might start, that doesn't mean you won't see a lefty that day. Prepare yourself for every game. And practice your bunting. You never know when you'll be called on for a suicide squeeze or to sacrifice a runner to second in hopes of breaking a tight game.

Switch-Hitting

Even in batting practice I've always been fascinated by switch hitters, how they can hit line drives from one side, then turn around and hit the same shots from the other side. I can't emphasize enough to young kids and parents the edge a switch hitter has in a game. I would recommend it to any young hitter. Not only does it increase your chance of playing, but, more important, if you're struggling from one side of the plate, chances are the next day you'll be able to turn around and try it from the other side.

How early should a player consider switch-hitting? My estimate is around eight years old, though you certainly could start a bit earlier, working off a tee. But by eight, the player's been given a chance to develop the basic skills. The best ways to teach switch-hitting are with a batting tee or by softly tossing a ball to the player from each side. I'd start out with 20 pitches a day from each side if the player is young, gradually working up to 10 or 15 minutes a day. One thing I've always found intriguing about switch-hitting is how someone can hit .290 from, say, the right side and just .230 from the left. Obviously, this begs the question, why not hit right all the time? The answers are fairly obvious: one, chances are you'll be platooned against right-handers, and two, you won't see the same pitches batting solely right-handed as you would switch-hitting.

So what do most hitters do who hit 60 points less from one side than the other? Sadly, not much. Typically, when you see them working out in the batting cage, they're hitting from their best side, saving the last 20 percent for the "off-side." That won't work. It's just like anything else in baseball: If you can't handle hot shots in the hole at short, you get a coach or friend to hit you a hundred ground balls a day to your right until you can. If you can't handle the slider or fastball from your weak side, you work on it until you can. You've got to organize your life to allow for more practice from that side. If that means getting to practice an hour early, so be it.

Each day, when practicing switch-hitting, you should aim to alternate from each side. Never take all your swings from one side in anticipation of facing a right-hander or a left-hander. All it

A good way to warm up or to practice your mechanics is by playing soft toss. Soft toss is a progression from the tee because you can hit a moving ball. Alternating with a partner, have him or her softly toss you the ball underhand, as we are doing in the picture. Keep your head on the ball and practice mechanics and making good contact.

takes is one signal to the bullpen from the manager to alter those plans. Also, take BP as a lefty off a lefty. This helps you prepare for pitches that move into your body—screwballs and two-seam fastballs—and pitches in the same location with similar spin that you would get from a right-hander.

Should you swing the same from both sides? Definitely not. These are two separate swings, two separate hitters, and should be treated as such. The switch hitter who displays power from both sides is rare. Mickey Mantle was an exception. So was Eddie Murray of Baltimore, who had two diametrically opposed stances and could take you deep from either side, just like the Yankees' Mark Teixeira today. But most of you considering switch-hitting or who are switch-hitting right now must come to grips with the kind of hitter you are from each side. Power from the right? Fine. More a line-drive hitter from the left? Great. Work on hitting the ball back up the middle, using your hands, cutting down on the swing.

Whatever the package, it's important not to forget fundamentals: the weight shift, the hands, the rhythm of the stride and swing. In some ways, switch-hitting may double the workload and frustration, but when that work pays off—and it will—it could make the difference between sitting and starting, and eventually, in some cases, the minors or the major leagues.

Conditioning

Because hitting combines the physical and the mental, the ability of your body to recognize and react to game situations makes a big difference in your performance. This has become more obvious in recent years, with the advent of large salaries in pro baseball. In the old days, conditioning began on the first day of spring training and ended on the last day of the season; today it's a year-round job. The result is that players are playing longer at higher levels of achievement. You only have to look at some recent statistics to prove that point.

At 37 in 1985, Carlton Fisk was one of baseball's top home-run hitters. At 44, Pete Rose broke Ty Cobb's all-time hit record and was still hitting around .270. Mariano Rivera was an all-star and one of the top, if not the best, closers in the majors in his late thirties and into his forties. I hit .339 the year I turned 38. Why? Well, I can assure you it wasn't performance-enhancing drugs. Conditioning, and overcoming the popular notion that just because you're pushing 40—or on the other side of it—you can't play anymore. Most of you reading this book won't have to worry about the age factor for quite a while, but you can just as easily get out of shape, and that will affect your abilities as a hitter.

Hitting combines the physical with the mental. Whatever you do, don't just jump into the box and start hitting. Give yourself enough time to warm up. Hitting requires every part of the body working together. Stretching and core work is especially important.

The first thing I'm going to ask of you is to stay away from drugs, cigarettes, smokeless tobacco, and alcohol. I'm very concerned about the drug and alcohol problem, not only in the major leagues but in our colleges and schools as well. I've watched players with all-star talents have their skills drastically reduced by alcohol and drugs. It really doesn't make any difference whether you're a great player or a great fan; those substances can ravage your body and ruin your life. Do yourself a favor: stay off drugs and booze.

I'm no fan of cigarettes, either. Aside from the long-term possibilities of lung cancer, the immediate effects of shortness of breath and reduced circulation are very detrimental to a player in a game built on speed. Hitting and fielding a baseball is hard enough; you need every physical advantage you can muster. So don't give up that edge. Instead, work to excel through conditioning and proper nutrition.

Here is an example of do as I say, not as I did. Not only is chewing smokeless tobacco a disgusting habit, it's a proven cause of all sorts of cancers. I wish I had never started chewing, and honestly, if you take one thing from this book, I hope it's to stay away from drugs and alcohol.

Another problem for ballplayers is curfew. After college, most clubs don't have one. I realize that with scheduling nowadays, with many games played at night and ending near 10:00 p.m., it's tough to go right home and rest. You want to party. But be careful. What you do at night affects how you play the next day. If you're tired, hung-over, or worried about a girl, it's going to keep you from concentrating on the job at hand.

When I was in the minor leagues, I didn't have much of a life off the field. First, I was intent on playing the game. Second, I never drank, so I played ping-pong, went to dinner, relaxed. I'd suggest the same for you. The minor leagues are full of players with the talent to play in the big leagues but, unfortunately, not the discipline. It's tough to say no sometimes, but it's a sacrifice you have to make if you want to be a better player.

There are many things you can do to keep your weight down and stay in shape. For the most part, a comfortable mixture of light weights, stretching exercises, running, and good nutrition will do it. Since you're not training for a triathlon, you really don't need much more than 30 minutes of exercise a day. During the offseason especially, find an activity or sequence of activities you enjoy and go to it! Here are some of my favorites:

Walking

I'm really not a big fan of jogging or distance running. In the past I ran for exercise quite a bit, but I stopped because the constant pounding was taking a toll on my knees and lower back. Three or four days a week, during the offseason and sometimes during the season, I would go off on a very brisk 15- or 20-minute walk along a nice, safe route near my home in Southern California. I think you'll find you get as much exercise from a brisk walk as you do from a long, slow jog, with less wear and tear on your body. I would do this for half of the week. The other half I would do the following:

Wind Sprints

Never my favorite exercise, but important for building wind and conditioning your legs for a long season. When you start alternate-day wind sprints, don't make it any more unpleasant than necessary. Start easy. Go out to a nearby track or the outfield of your baseball field and mark off 50 yards. That's long enough. Start off by doing

No one likes sprints less than I do, but I appreciate how important lower-body strength is to good hitting. You don't need to run wind sprints every day, but do get your sprint work in.

five to seven easy wind sprints. Sprint one way and walk the return route, taking deep breaths in and out. Minimize the stress on your legs by wearing good, comfortable training shoes rather than your cleats. After several days, start building up to 10, then 15 sprints by adding one a day on your sprint days. Work on your speed and improve your ability to maintain good speed throughout all 15 sprints.

Basketball and Racquet Sports

Because not everyone lives in a year-round warm climate, it's important to find activities you can do indoors. Basketball, racquetball, and tennis were always three of my favorites because they involve constant motion, are good for your wind, demand split-second reactions and decisions, and increase your hand–eye coordination and foot speed, all of which help keep your mind and body sharp for hitting.

Weights

One look at me now or in my playing days will tell you I was not going to win any Mr. Universe contests, but I do believe in weight training. If you are going to work with weights, stick to flexibility exercises, developing the parts of the body important to your hitting—arms, wrists, forearms. Do three sets of 10 to 15 repetitions. And don't increase the weight until you can do all three sets. Baseball is a game of quick starts and stops, and flexibility reduces the risk of muscle pulls. You don't want to bulk up, but you do want to be strong.

Hand Exercises

Someone who preaches hand hitting as much as I do is going to suggest you have to keep your hands strong. The old "squeezing a tennis ball" exercise has almost become a cliché, but it really does help to strengthen your hands and wrists. And it's so easy to do. I would squeeze a tennis ball when I was walking around the house or just sitting and watching TV. I got to the point where half the time I wasn't even aware I was doing it.

By now you've read over and over how important hands are to good hitting. The reliable old squeeze-a-tennis-ball exercise is a good way to build the wrist and forearm strength needed to build strong hands and create good bat speed. You can do this drill sitting in front of the TV. Take every opportunity you can to become a better hitter.

Playing in Pain

My attitude is that if you're hurt, the only person who can make the decision to play or not is you. Sure, broken legs are broken legs, but with ankle sprains and hamstring or groin pulls, once the team trainer clears you, the decision is yours. Personally, I wouldn't play with an injury if I honestly felt playing would cause the team more harm than good. I watched for years as Tony Oliva tried one machine, one cream, one shot after another to get his ravaged legs into shape. Six, sometimes seven hours a day of work in the training room. Home remedies. Once he even tried rubbing a can of STP oil treatment on his knee. But Tony never quit; he *wanted* to play, and because of his desire, his influence on a young ballplayer like myself was immense. It helped me realize that if there's any way you can get on that field, go for it. But, on the other hand, don't be stupid. If you can't play at a respectable level, sit down, rest a spell, and let your body recover. In the long run, you're doing both yourself and your teammates a big favor.

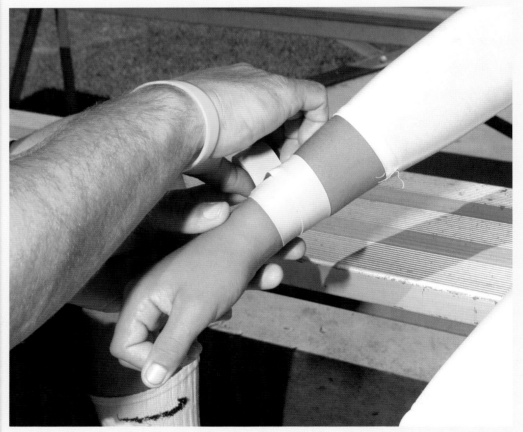

When you get injured, don't keep secrets—get treatment. When you are tired or hurt, quantity of motion takes over for quality of motion, and bad swing habits can get ingrained into your muscle memory. The science of sports medicine has never been better. Take advantage of it.

When I was playing baseball on an exhibition tour in Japan many years ago, I learned an exercise the Japanese use to help develop hand strength. This exercise utilizes uncooked rice. Take your hands and insert them, one at a time, in a deep bucket of rice, squeeze the rice, and release. Do five repetitions of 10 squeezes on a regular basis and you'll feel the difference in your hands, wrists, and forearms.

Another good exercise to help you increase hand strength can be done in your living room. Spread newspaper on the floor and get on all fours. Open your hand as wide as you can and place it in the middle of the spread-out newspaper. Then start squeezing the newspaper, wadding it until you have gathered the entire sheet in your hand.

One additional exercise for your hands is table tennis, which really places a premium on hand–eye coordination. It is important to always try to play with someone better than you are. Force yourself to play up to his or her level. You will see your own improvement, and it will help your hitting.

Traditional Exercises

Those exercises that everyone hates and take for granted in phys ed class are great conditioners. I'm talking about push-ups, chin-ups, and especially sit-ups. You can have the fastest hands in the world, but if you have a soft, unresponsive stomach, you're not going to be able to get your hips into action. So do 50 or 100 sit-ups a day.

Play Ball

One of the best ways to stay in shape for baseball is to play the game. Swing the bat; take ground balls; shag fly balls whenever you can. Don't worry about swinging a weighted bat a hundred times a day. Weighted bats should be used only to help you loosen up. Swing *your* bat. Take batting practice and play ball. That is what's going to help you build bat speed.

Proper Diet

My wife, Rhonda, will laugh every time she looks at this page and sees that I'm writing about proper diet. You see, she knows that I have a sweet tooth and enjoy my share of blueberry muffins and Snickers bars. But that's okay. I think it's important to mix fun foods into your diet on an occasional basis. Just keep in mind the four basic food groups—dairy, meat and fish, fruits and vegetables, and breads and cereals. You have to build your diet around the above groups, but, to my mind, you don't have to be a fanatic. Enjoy your foods, and if you overdo it one day, cut back a little the next day. I mean, I never met a lemon cake I didn't like.

Have you ever heard the noise a highly tuned car engine makes when it gets cheap fuel? Not very pleasant, is it? Like that car, your body is your engine. You need to practice good eating habits to keep your engine purring. Learn how your body reacts to food, and don't eat too much on game days.

I understand and respect the need for good nutrition as well as anyone, but I am not a fanatic. Every once in a while it's okay to mix in some fun foods; just don't overdo it. My personal favorites are blueberry muffins and Snickers bars.

Though I like to have fun with my diet, I increased my discipline to its absolute highest level on game days. Everybody is different, but if you eat too much *before* a game, you're going to be sluggish *during* the game. I preferred to eat light about four hours before game time and play the game slightly hungry. This pre-game meal can be something as simple as a sandwich or fruit before a night game or breakfast before a day game. Then, after the game, I'll have my big meal of steak, chicken, or fish, plus vegetables and salad.

During a game, the important thing is to replenish the fluid levels in your body. Stay away from carbonated beverages and lean toward the Gatorade-type drinks most teams now have—or, better yet, water. But be careful. Don't drink too much and get bloated to the point where it's going to hurt you on the field.

As far as vitamins are concerned, take a multivitamin if you like, but it's really not necessary. Find a nice combination of foods from the four basic food groups. Eat well on a daily basis and you'll get all the vitamins and nutrition you need.

Your body is made up of mostly water. Hydration before, during, and after a game is critical for the body to function at maximum effectiveness. Water is always great, and there is also a wide selection of sport drinks fortified with electrolytes.

Chapter 9

Teaching Hitting

The best way to encourage a player's participation and growth is to keep the game fun.

To be a good teacher you have to know what you're talking about. I'm afraid too many coaches today are frustrated ex-jocks who think they know the game but really don't. Yet they demand that a young, impressionable hitter conform to their style of hitting. I would insist that if you want to be a good hitting teacher, you must first seek out and learn the fundamentals of good hitting. You don't necessarily have to be able to physically perform what you're teaching, but you must be acutely aware of just what your beliefs are, how they work together to form important concepts, and know how to explain these concepts clearly and concisely.

Therefore, if you are serious about being a good teacher, you must invest the time necessary to increase your knowledge about the game. In every community there are many college coaches, pro coaches, or ex-pro ballplayers who know good hitting. Seek them out. Talk to them. Find out what they have to say about hitting and apply it to your own teaching.

That's just the first step. I'm also a big believer in clinics and seminars. Any youth organization that hires its own coaches should take the responsibility of educating them. The best seminars and clinics are hands-on sessions given by experienced, professional coaches. By "hands-on" I mean "more than talk." I like to see student teachers on the field, learning for themselves what they should be teaching.

Once you've been to the clinics, it's important to put into action what you've learned. You don't go to a clinic to fortify

Knowledge is important in a teacher, but the ability to communicate that information is just as important. Remember as a teacher to understand the level of the player you are communicating with. Keep your message precise and your terminology consistent.

your own theories; you go to refine and expand and sometimes even unlearn them. Keep an open mind.

The importance of observation can't be overlooked. If you are fortunate enough to live in a city with a major or minor league team, get out to the park as often as possible. Don't just show up at game time and watch nine innings. Get out early enough to watch batting practice. If there is no professional franchise nearby, travel to the local university or community college. Watch those players; introduce yourself to the coach; talk baseball. You'll be surprised how pleasant these people can be if you hit them at the right time, after a practice or around the cage during hitting drills on an off-day (definitely not 30 minutes before a game).

Learning doesn't end on the field. There is a lot of great literature on the game. Some of it is older and time-tested. Other books are new and improved!

Coaches should read a variety of hitting books as well as watch video on hitting. By watching a role model perform picture-perfect skills, your nervous system processes and adjusts the input until the goal state is realized and maintained. I believe that video technology is *the* most important discovery in teaching hitting since hard work.

Major league teams have video operators who tape every at bat of every game, should the players care to view them. Tony Gwynn of the Padres took it a step further. His wife, Alicia, went out to the ballpark each night and taped every one of his at bats. After the ballgame Tony would go straight home to view the tape and evaluate his mechanics. It's no accident that Tony was a batting champion, a Hall of Famer, and went on to teach the game as the coach at his alma mater, San Diego State.

Another former batting champion, Keith Hernandez of the Mets, was taught to hit by his father, who taped all his games off cable television. During the 1985 season Keith's dad noticed from one of the tapes that Keith had altered his stance so drastically that his father, looking from a center-field camera angle, couldn't read the number on Keith's back during his setup. A long-distance telephone call followed, and Keith almost immediately broke out of the worst slump of his career and moved his batting average up to the .300 mark. He finished at .309 with 91 RBI. When we were home, I'd sometimes watch myself on tape two or three times a week following ballgames, just to make sure I had not lapsed into any bad habits.

My point is that, with the tremendous growth of technology, every serious batting instructor should have video in his or her teaching equipment. If you're a high school coach, urge your school to purchase the needed equipment. If you're a Little League coach, there's a good chance that at least one set of parents out of an entire team will own a video camera.

One of the big advantages players have today is being able to watch themselves on video or DVD. The great Tony Gwynn spent almost as much time in front of a monitor as he did in the batter's box.

The best vantage point from which to have your swing taped is directly in front of you (the pitcher's point of view). Next best is directly from the side.

The nice thing about taping youngsters hitting is that not only will they hear your instruction, but they'll be able to grasp what you're telling them more quickly because they can see themselves as well. It allows the youngsters to sit and watch themselves hit, see what they need to improve on, and learn from what they do well.

The two ideal viewing angles for videotaping a hitter are from in front of him and from the side facing him; that is, from the first-base side if you're taping a right-handed hitter and from the third-base side if you're taping a lefty. By shooting from the side or front of the hitter, you can see more than you can from any other angle. In front is the best, but it is obviously impractical in a game situation. And make sure you have the hitter in the picture from head to toe so you can observe all the body parts in action.

If you have unlimited access to a video camera, tape both practice and game situations. If access is limited, tape just the game at bats. During a game situation we can see how the added mental pressures affect the player's concentration at the plate. A player will more typically show the imperfections of his hitting style in a game situation than in batting practice.

Evaluating a Hitter and Adjusting

The first thing you must keep in mind is that each hitter is an individual and must be evaluated as an individual.

Rod Carew couldn't hit exactly like Joe Mauer, who couldn't hit like Tony Gwynn, who couldn't hit like George Brett. We all have found our own elements of style and comfort within the basic fundamentals of good hitting. Each hitter should experiment and find his own comfortable style of hitting. And a good hitting instructor should give the player enough freedom to develop his own style. Billy Martin says that he never really believed in hitting coaches until he worked with Lou Piniella. That's because Lou took a customized approach to each hitter. Thus, your biggest challenge as a teacher will be understanding that each hitter's style is unique. You have to watch each hitter without preconceived notions. When he's going good, what is he doing and why? When he's going bad, you have to be able to answer the same questions.

As I touched upon earlier, the best place to observe a hitter is from directly in front of him. In front of the hitter you can see everything: hand movements, head positioning, the stride (is he stepping out too soon?), a loose front shoulder. Facing a hitter head-on also allows you to see if the hitter has fear of the ball. Most youngsters fear being hit by a pitch. They don't want to get hit, so instead of watching the ball and swinging aggressively they'll have a tendency to bail out a little and not take their best swing. In a case like this you have to try to assure them that they are going to get hit at times, and that it will hurt. But the hurt will go away.

The most important thing I tell youngsters when I do clinics is to learn how to swing the bat, to be aggressive, and to make consistent contact. Don't worry about getting hit with the baseball, and don't think too much when you're at the plate.

If a player continues to cringe or steps into the bucket when the ball approaches the plate, refer to page 18 for drills designed to conquer this fear. Part of the fear of being hit is overcoming the fear of the ball's approaching impact. This drill allows the hitter to familiarize his mind and body to the sight and feel of the ball hitting him, helping him overcome a major obstacle.

Now, if a player continually steps in the bucket, it is best to take him back to the basics. Start him off on a batting tee. Tell him to concentrate on one thing: keeping his head on the ball. You can even make a mark on the ground in front of him and have him concentrate on striding into the mark and keeping his head on the ball. Once he seems to be adjusting to that, advance to a soft underhand toss from about 10 feet away. Again, have your hitter repeat the process of striding into the ball while keeping his head still and on the ball throughout the swing. This will help program the proper mechanics into the player's memory bank, so that come game time all the drills will pay off.

The Batting Tee and the GAP Hitter

We just talked about using the batting tee to help overcome the fundamental problem of stepping into the bucket. Like the use of video, the batting tee and the GAP (game and practice) Hitter are essential equipment for any good coach.

In many respects, the batting tee is the Rodney Dangerfield of baseball equipment: it doesn't get any respect. But it does from Rod Carew. Kids laugh at the batting tee as being elementary. But that's how you learn, how you teach—by breaking hitting down to its simplest, most fundamental form.

The tee is so good because it allows young hitters to work on their mechanics. You can work on hitting the ball to the opposite field and practice pulling the ball off the tee, and stride we've already talked about. One of the things to keep in mind when you're practicing off a tee is that the ball is stationary. The player should adjust his stance in relation to the tee, not vice versa. You don't want to have your players practice pulling the ball from the same position that they use to practice going to the opposite field. An outside pitch goes the opposite way; the inside

There is no substitution for live pitching, but there are a lot of great training aids out there that allow hitters to practice on their own. One of my favorites is the GAP Hitter. The GAP Hitter combines the best elements of soft toss and the batting tee. I expect someday it will replace the tee in youth competitions.

pitch is a pitch you pull. Move the tee for an outside strike when your hitter is practicing going the other way and inside for pulling the ball. Remind your players of the fundamentals—hands, weight shift, stride. You can't lose sight of the basics or your mistakes will ultimately be passed along to your players.

The GAP Hitter is the most effective tool for developing and refining hitting mechanics that I've ever seen, as it offers a moving ball that increases a young player's hand–eye coordination and can help advanced players hone their skills by practicing situational hitting.

It was developed through several iterations and tested by numerous players and teams from the youth level to the pros. With a ball secured to a patented ball attachment that is connected to a tether hanging from a pendulum, the GAP Hitter allows a player to hit a moving ball at all positions within the strike zone. Unlike many hitting aids, the mechanism releases the ball at contact and, by doing so, provides the batter instant feedback on the direction, speed, and trajectory of the batted ball.

Hall of Famer Roy Campanella used to say, "You have to have a lot of little boy in you to play this game." I couldn't agree more. Work hard, but have fun doing it.

Playing Is More Important than Winning

Back when my daughter played in a Bobby Sox Softball league, in order to have an official game you had to complete seven innings within a two-hour time limit or the game was replayed. One day, with time running out and my daughter's team in a comfortable lead, it became obvious that the kids would never finish the game in the allotted time. Rather than accept that, her coach sent her and her teammates up to the plate with the instruction to make an out.

I was quite upset. I don't want kids to learn that you have to win at all costs. And as a hitter, seeing kids swinging at pitches over their heads or in the dirt for the express purpose of making an out made me shudder.

Good coaches teach good hitting and good hitting practices. You teach your players to be hitters by letting them hit. Hear me: *a walk is not as good as a hit in Little League.* If a kid works a walk while aggressively looking for a base hit, that's good hitting. If a kid goes up to the plate with an 0-0 count hoping for a walk, that's bad coaching.

Unfortunately, there are poor coaches at the Little League level, but you don't have to be one, and you don't have to be quiet if you see one in your league. Fortunately, most Little Leagues have instituted a rule that makes it mandatory for each child to play a specified number of innings in each game. If your league doesn't have that rule, work to get one introduced.

As a coach, you must understand that the best way to encourage a player's participation and growth is to keep it fun. When players stop having fun, they quit, especially at a younger age. Most Little Leaguers probably won't even play high school baseball, much less college or professional. Let your players get the most from their ability and help them along the way. Don't favor one eight-year-old over another because he or she may have better skills. Let them all be exposed to competition, but expose them, too, to a spirit of equality, fairness, and teamwork. Many kids are quiet and shy, and the only time they can really enjoy themselves is on the field. Don't take away a young player's dignity so you can win a game.

Praise and Criticism

We've identified three of the major tools necessary to build great hitters: work hard, video, and the proper teaching equipment. There is another major tool you should make use of, and that's praise. I think you should constantly praise young hitters, and I don't think you should ever criticize them. A pat on the back is great, no matter how old you are, whether you're a Little Leaguer or a big-leaguer.

A good teacher is firm but fair. Remember that nothing reinforces good teaching as well as praise. It's crucial to let young players know when they have performed well and equally important to end each session on a positive note.

Nothing makes you want to work harder than recognition for a job well done. You should also give your players a pat on the back when they don't do well. Reassure them. If they made an out, they'll get another at bat and another after that. Young hitters discourage easily. Good teachers reassure; they don't criticize.

Since I retired I've been to quite a few Little League games. I was embarrassed, upset, and angry, not just at the coaches but at the parents. Children should have the opportunity to go out and have fun and compete with other kids. Don't pressure them from the stands with words like "You're not going to watch any television tonight if you strike out or make a bad play." I think that when you're coaching young kids, instead of berating youngsters when they make a bad play, you should give them a pat on the fanny. Let them know you're on their side. Don't belabor a bad play; teach the kids so they learn, so they want to play harder. Make sure they understand why it's a bad play and show them how to do it correctly the next time. The best time to correct a player's mistake is directly following the at bat or error. If the player pulled his or her head, tell the kid while it's fresh in his or her mind—and in yours. But do it in such a way that the player is reassured of being one step closer to being a good hitter and confident in his or her ability as a player and a person.

There is always enough credit to go around. Make sure your players understand that good hitting is a means to an end (victory). There are plenty of ways to help a team win. I would rather go 0-2 with a sac fly and win than go 2-3 with a home run and lose. Good teammates root for their teammates to succeed because when they succeed, you succeed.

Parents are more involved in the game these days than ever before. Good communication with parents can hold off a lot of potential problems. Make sure you never let a conflict with a parent surface publicly. Parental investment is a good thing, but maintain the lines of authority and *always* be the adult.

Coping with Overzealous Parents

Possibly one of the most difficult aspects of coaching young players is overzealous parents. Needless to say, each parent puts his or her child's interests above the rest; it's only natural. But unfortunately some parents take it too far. I think it's important from the start that you make the parents understand, as tactfully as possible, that once the teams are selected, the team is your responsibility. Talk to them about participation, the spirit of teamwork, and the importance of praise. Let them know that winning isn't everything to you, but developing these players is. If they can't accept that, maybe their child should play for another team.

Most important, don't ever let a personality conflict with a parent surface publicly in front of the other players or their parents, whether it be at the ballpark, a community function, or a gathering at your house. Take it upon yourself to be the mature, rational part of the equation.

If you're a young player or the parent of one, it's important for you to look for the above attributes in your coach or your child's coach. If you're not satisfied that the coach has your or your child's best interests at heart, you should discuss it with the coach. If that has no impact, talk it over at home. If the player is unhappy with a coach for justifiable reasons, consider changing teams—or sports—until the problem can be rectified.

Summary

A good teacher is hard to find. I only had one in my career, and that's Tony Oliva, a three-time American League batting champion. The reason Tony was such a great coach is that he understands athletes and has every one of the following attributes:

- Knowledge of hitting and the ability to communicate that knowledge

- Awareness that each hitter is an individual and the ability to familiarize himself with each individual hitter

- Realization that his job is to help each hitter reach his potential

- Confidence, strength in his own knowledge of hitting, and respect for every player's capacity to learn

Finally, my philosophy is that to be successful, you have to be willing to make mistakes and to learn from those mistakes. Most coaches went through the same problems and made the same mistakes as children growing up, and they can also make mistakes as adults. You know youngsters are going to make mistakes, and you can be there to correct those mistakes, to praise the children. You're not there to chew them out or to sit them down on the bench because they walked up and struck out in a situation where they should have gotten a base hit. Sometimes you have to raise your voice, but you'll get more out of your players with praise and a firm set of standards than you will with intimidation.

There is no such thing as a born hitter. Everyone needs a mentor. Mine was Tony Oliva, who took me under his wing when I was a rookie in 1967 and later became my roommate. Tony was a great hitter in his own right and won three American League batting titles in the 1960s. I am hopeful that someday Tony will join me as a member of the Baseball Hall of Fame. *Hannah Foslien/Getty Images*

Chapter 10

Carew on the Game's Great Hitters

Baseball continues to change in many ways over the years, but a good hitter is a good hitter no matter what era. In the game today there are four hitters who stand out to me as being not only among the best, but also as my favorites to watch play the game. With plenty of big numbers, batting titles and all-star selections, Joe Mauer, Albert Pujols, José Reyes, and Ichiro Suzuki are, in my opinion, the best of the best. Let's take a closer look at each of these great hitters.

Joe Mauer

Joe is one of the best hitters in baseball because both his mental and physical approaches to the game are right on. Mentally, he always stays within himself and takes what the pitcher and defense give him. I have heard people criticize Joe because he doesn't hit more home runs, but he always hits the ball hard and that's what I care about. He also has enough pop to hit the ball out when the situation calls for it. Joe's hitting mechanics are very simple. His stride is short and powerful. Joe triggers his swings with his hips, but he is careful not to open those hips too quickly. He stays back on the ball well and still hits the ball far enough in front of the plate to generate power and get great extension. My guess is that Joe will add to his three batting titles before his career is over.

Albert Pujols

It's amazing to me that Albert Pujols (or anyone) could hit more than 400 home runs in his first 10 seasons in the major leagues. But when you look at Albert's swing it's not really all that surprising. Albert transmits power from head to toe, literally. Albert's hips and hands are in total synch with each other. He cocks his hips and hands at the exact same time and moves them into the ball on the swing in total harmony. That controlled swing and knowledge of the strike zone give him good power to all fields. Pujols makes a great turn with his back leg and hits off a really firm front leg. He has great extension and holds that extension without losing balance. His head is solid; all that power rotates around his head.

José Reyes

I really like this guy. He knows how to hit. José does a great job of using the whole field when he hits. I have watched with interest as this switch hitter gets better and better. He's a natural righty, but his lower body is more flexible from the left side, so I think you will see continued improvement in his average from that side. José can sometimes be a little aggressive at the plate, but as he continues to mature he will get more and more selective, and that too will make him an even tougher out. There is nothing

I love watching José Reyes hit the ball into the gaps and leg out those triples. Reyes has some pop, which I like, but what I like most about him is that his approach to hitting is the same from the left side as it is from the right side. *Jim McIsaac/Getty Images*

Had he spent his entire career in the major leagues, Ichiro might have surpassed 4,000 hits. Two hundred or more hits in each of his first 10 years in the big leagues is an amazing accomplishment. *Otto Greule Jr./Getty Images*

more exciting to me than watching José leg out a triple. If he hasn't already won a batting title by the time you read this, his time is coming.

Ichiro Suzuki

Ever since I made a run at hitting .400 back in 1977, people have asked, "Can anyone hit .400 in this day and age?" Truth is, if anyone is going to hit .400 it will be a player like Ichiro. He makes great contact, gets the ball in play, can hit to all fields, and gets his share of infield and bunt base hits. People make a lot of Ichiro moving when he hits, but you will notice that his first move is always toward the pitcher, and his weight and his hands stay back. Two hundred plus hits for 10 consecutive seasons is a remarkable accomplishment, especially when you are playing for a team that is not in a pennant race—a time when it's harder for some players to stay interested. Another thing I have admired about Ichiro is his extensive stretching routine. That flexibility has served him well, especially in the later years of his career. Had Ichiro played his entire career in the United States, his hit totals might have been staggering. I am holding a place for Ichiro in both the 3,000-hit club and the National Baseball Hall of Fame.

Looking Back

Five of the best hitters in baseball at the time I was concluding my career and, for the most part, into the 1990s were, in alphabetical order, Wade Boggs of Boston, KC's George Brett, Tony Gwynn of the Padres, the Yankees' Don Mattingly, and Eddie Murray of Baltimore. They won an abundance of batting titles, and five of the six have been enshrined in Cooperstown. Brett, Mattingly, and Murray combined power with their ability to make contact. And they used the whole field. Their power came from natural strength, plus a slightly uppercut swing. Boggs, Gwynn, and I had flatter swings that complemented our line-drive approach to hitting.

I analyzed each of these players at the height of their careers, and my technical evaluations remain much the same today.

Wade Boggs was one of the most disciplined hitters I ever saw. That discipline paid off with six batting titles, 3,000 hits, and a plaque in Cooperstown. *Ron Vesely/MLB Photos via Getty Images*

Wade Boggs

The most disciplined hitter to come into the American League in years, Wade had an idea of what he wanted to do every time he came to the plate—not to mention the discipline, the ability to wait for a pitch. Because of his discipline, you couldn't pitch to Wade any one way. He could lay off pitches that weren't *exactly* where he wanted them. I don't think there was any pitcher in the American League he couldn't handle. It took Wade a few years to receive the recognition he deserved, but he ultimately ended up in Cooperstown with the baseball greats. He was a quiet player who just went out and got his one or two hits every day.

Because of his discipline, Wade took a rap for not hitting certain pitches in certain situations. He was accused of always waiting for *the* perfect pitch, but he knew himself as a hitter. Each hitter has to find himself at the plate, and Wade found what worked for him. I also understand that much was written about Wade's not driving in runs. I'm sensitive to this, because the same was said about me. But hitting is something you do for the team to help it win. Wade never knocked in a bunch of runs batting first or second in the lineup. But during a full season, a good ball club will score around 800 runs; during that season, Wade Boggs would often score 100 runs and drive in another 70 or 80. That means he had a hand in 150 of his team's 800 runs, nearly 20 percent. A player who does what the ball club needs when they need it. That's how I measure a hitter.

Wade won five batting titles in his career, including four in a row from 1985 to 1988. His first, in 1983, kept me from winning my eighth. I hit .339 that year, good enough to win most years, but it wasn't even close to Wade's .361.

George Brett

A thinking man's hitter. A pitcher could never throw George the same pitch two or three times in a row, because George would adjust and take advantage of a pitch thrown once too often. George set up with his weight back, and used a more pronounced closed front toe to help him stay in. He had a great approach into the ball, used his hands well, and hit the ball to the opposite field as well as anyone. Because of his great hands and hitting knowledge, you rarely saw George fooled by a pitch. He was also a very, very aggressive hitter. And that made George even tougher in clutch situations.

There is one other interesting thing hitters can learn from George Brett. In the prime of his career, in 1984, George "slumped" to .284 and 13 home runs. It was a year George played injured and maybe had some problems with his weight. George did sometimes play hurt, perhaps even to the detriment of his team, although his intentions were otherwise. He never let his off year affect him, although some foolishly questioned his desire. There are years you will be injured and years you'll hit the ball hard but right at someone. George had that kind of year in 1984. But in watching him that year, I noticed George still had the good mechanics going for him. I knew he'd be back and expected him to have a big year in 1985. He did.

Tony Gwynn

Since he played in the National League, I didn't see as much of Tony as I did of the others. But I did see Tony in spring training, on television, and on videotape, and he was impressive. Like Boggs and me, he used his hands exceptionally well. In particular, Tony did a good job of taking the inside pitch to the left side. I'd say he was in the same category of hitting as I was. When I saw Tony, it seemed he had the up-the-middle/opposite field idea going through his mind at all times. He also worked a pitcher very well. His hand action let him spoil a lot of good pitches and extended his time at bat until he could get a good pitch to hit. That's the sign of a good hitter.

I also noticed how Tony wiggled his bat behind his head when he was set in the batter's box. This is not something that coaches teach, but it underscores what this book is all about—finding out what works for you. Tony's bat wiggle helped him to stay loose, but it also served as a timing mechanism to start his swing.

I lived in Anaheim, only 60 miles from San Diego, and I noticed that Tony got quite a bit of publicity in 1985, after hitting .351 to lead the league the year before. I read often how people, Tony included, were disappointed that he dropped off to the low .300s in 1985 (he finished the season at .317). You can't hit .351 each year. If you can hit .300 year in and year out, you're a great hitter, because it gets harder every year you're in the league. And that's just what Gwynn did, racking up a remarkable eight batting titles by the time he retired.

Don Mattingly

Early in his career, Don was the best young hitter I'd seen in a long time. He was the type of hitter who really stayed within himself. He had good power and used the whole field. In late 1985 Don went on a hitting tear that was unbelievable. While everyone noticed all the home runs, the thing that impressed me the most was all the singles and doubles to the opposite field. Don never went away from the basics during his hot streak. He hit the ball well to *all* fields and was not easily fooled, making him a tough out at all times. He was so confident at the plate that you could just feel it in the field. Like me, he knew he was good, and he wanted the pitcher to know it. Don was the only other player I've seen make major adjustments to his stance during a game. The episode against Candelaria, mentioned earlier, illustrates this point. Like most of the hitters we're talking about, Don started with his weight on his back leg. His closed front toe was similar to Brett's. And like George, he had a slightly uppercut swing.

I always liked the way Don handled himself as a person and as a hitter. Even when he was a young guy, it was as though he'd been in the league 10 years.

Don Mattingly always says I was his favorite hitter and he patterned himself after me. I am very flattered, but Don hit for more power than I did without sacrificing contact. Injuries probably cost him a place in the Hall of Fame, but Donnie Baseball's legacy as one of the greatest Yankees of all time cannot be denied. *Ronald C. Modra/Sports Imagery/ Getty Images*

Eddie Murray was the best hitter in baseball for about 10 years. This switch hitter was dangerous from either side of the plate. Eddie hit for power and average, as his 504 home runs and 3,255 hits show. A Hall of Famer for sure. *Mitchell Layton/Getty Images*

Eddie Murray

The best all-around hitter in baseball during his career, Eddie Murray was the Mickey Mantle of his time: a switch hitter with speed, power, and the ability to hit for average. Eddie was a tough hitter who would not let himself be fooled or intimidated by a pitcher. Knock him down and he got up twice as determined to beat you. He was one of those rare players who was able to "find themselves" from both sides of the plate. He seemed to have a little more power from the left side, but he could knock runs in from either side, as the Angels found out in 1985 when Eddie had nine RBI against us in one game.

Eddie had a good eye at the plate, was selective, and walked a lot. Even so, he was a very aggressive hitter, as you can see from his strikeout totals. In fact, Eddie's strikeout total dropped from 87 in 1984 to only 68 in 1985, while his home runs and RBI rose to 31 and 124.

In the prime of Murray's career, Boggs, Gwynn, and Mattingly were brilliant young players who had excelled in the early stages of their careers. But they were still relatively new to the big leagues. Eddie Murray had done it so well for so long from both sides of the plate, he was in a class by himself as a hitter.

Afterword

Carew on Carew

You could say I got a rolling start in life. It was October 1, 1945, and my mother was on a train headed for a clinic when she went into labor. Luckily, there was a nurse—who later became my godmother—on the train and she provided a helping hand or two. Hard to believe, but in appreciation of this woman's kindness, my mother seriously considered naming me Margaret Ann after her. Thankfully, there was a doctor aboard and he finished up the delivery. His name was Dr. Rodney Cline. I became Rodney Cline Carew. Can you imagine all the fights I would have had defending a name like Margaret Ann?

I spent my early years in Gatun, a little town of 2,000 near the Panama Canal. When you grow up in a Latin American country, especially in a small town, there really isn't much to do. We didn't have a swimming pool, so many of us ended up swimming in the canal, a dubious proposition because of the presence of alligators and ships slipping through the locks. Quite a few of my friends had accidents in the canal, so to keep out of harm's way we turned to sports—everything from volleyball to soccer.

Baseball, however, was my first love. I began playing at five, using an old broomstick for a bat. We were so poor that major league bats and balls were out of the question. So we improvised, painting broomsticks different colors, imitating our favorite American players (mine were Willie Mays and Jackie Robinson), playing out our fantasies in the streets, with tennis balls and paper bags for gloves. And if for some reason nobody wanted to play,

Writing this book was a great experience. Rewriting it 25 years later, after a second career as a major league hitting coach and youth clinician, has showed me that what worked for me as a hitter works as an instructor. I hope what has worked for me works for you. Happy hitting!

MVP Books Collection

I'd throw a ball against the steps of our apartment for hours, never stopping until dark.

Later on, when I was eight, we moved away from Gatun to Gamboa, a couple of miles south of the canal. Again, the lifestyle wasn't much, a five-room wooden apartment filled with my father, mother, brother, and two sisters. Like everyone else, I'm a product of my upbringing. I was a very sick child growing up—I had rheumatic fever—and my father never really thought I was tough enough. I was in and out of the hospital a lot, something that irritated him because he believed little boys should be tough (like my brother), so I was physically abused at times. I mean, there wasn't a time in my life I wasn't licked or punched or whipped, often for no reason whatsoever. Certainly I was good in school; I never caused my parents problems; I never fought. But for some reason my father chose to pick on me and, to be honest, it affected my personality. I think it's one reason I was so reticent with the press, so cautious about opening up to others. When you're young and under attack, you withdraw from family and friends. So shyness stays with you in later years.

As time went on, my mother kept in close contact with my godmother, who, it turns out, lived in New York. One day, when I was 14 or so, my godmother asked if I wanted to come to the United States and finish my education. I wanted to leave Panama at the time because I knew that after graduation from school most kids did very little. I didn't want to just exist, I wanted to be somebody, and I knew that if given half a chance, with my baseball activities, I could make something of myself after finishing high school in New York.

I'll never forget looking out the airplane window on my first trip to New York harbor. It was dark, the city aglow, a blaze of light; I had the feeling a whole new world was opening up to me. Sure, I was a little scared; I knew of the problems any person faces in New York—particularly someone just 14. But my mother was already there, so I adjusted quickly, learning the ropes, how to ride the subways, what buses to take, the dangers of being in the wrong place at the right time.

The one thing I can still remember both my mother and godmother drilling into my head was the danger of succumbing to peer pressure. I think that's one reason so many kids have problems today. They want to be liked, to fit in, so they follow the leader. But there are problems with following others. A lot of times you can end up staring at a dead end. Soon after immigrating to New York I enrolled at George Washington High School in the Bronx. I had a hard time learning English, spending so much time on the new language that I wasn't able to try out for the high school baseball team—and anyway, the coach had already told me to forget it, that I wasn't good enough to make his club. So I played sandlot ball instead, which was fine. It gave me the confidence I needed. I can still remember lying in my bed, listening to Armed Forces Radio at night, dreaming about the day I would play in Yankee Stadium or a World Series. The dream drove me, day after day, swing after swing. I knew if given half a chance I would make it—no matter what a high school coach had said. As time went on, scouts from a half-dozen teams—the Chicago Cubs, New York Yankees, Pittsburgh Pirates, and, of course, the Minnesota Twins—started showing up at my games. There was never any doubt in those days about what I wanted to do after high school: I wanted to sign. The sooner the better.

I'll never forget that signing day. It was graduation day in a lot of ways—from high school and from amateur baseball. I remember sitting at graduation ceremonies, staring at my watch every few seconds, thinking, "Let's get this thing over with right now." Sure enough, right after graduation, a Minnesota Twins scout took my uncle and me out to dinner. The scout asked how much it would take to get me to sign. I didn't care and said, "Let's just get this thing over with, because I'm ready to sign, get on an airplane, and play ball somewhere." But my uncle, thank goodness, had a more level head. He took me aside and said, "Let's find out the specifics of the contact." Once we did, I still couldn't write my name fast enough. I wanted to play ball.

Now, looking back on more than two decades of my professional career, certain memories do shine through. Certainly making an all-star team my first year was a highlight. Just standing on the same field with Ernie Banks, Mays, Mantle—men I had idolized—made my knees shake.

My biggest thrill, however, has to be my first major league hit! It came off Dave McNally of the Orioles on my second big-league at bat. I know it's hard to believe No. 3,000 doesn't top the list, but honestly, when you get that first hit it means you belong. You can relax. You proved you can play, even if it's only for the moment. I stayed around for quite some time, fortunately, but believe me, it's done nothing to diminish the excitement of that first base hit. My three thousandth hit? Well, just being mentioned in the same breath with Cobb, Mays, Roberto Clemente, and Pete Rose is almost as gratifying. After all, there are only 28 athletes in our little club, and I consider it an honor to be included in the membership.

Another honor related to that three thousandth hit came in November 1985, when I was asked by the government in Panama to return for a celebration. As part of the event I was given that nation's Medal of Honor by the Panamanian president, and my number—29—was permanently retired. That means no player, at any level and in any sport, can wear that number in Panama. It was a heartwarming experience for someone who has purposely kept his Panamanian citizenship in hopes of giving the youth of that country a role model. The sights and sounds of that trip will never be forgotten.

One thing I'm often asked during interviews is what I've learned from my time in the game, what experience I would like to share with others. One thing I certainly discovered was the importance of humility. Unlike most doctors, lawyers, and teachers, athletes perform in the full view of the press and public. Often our achievements—no more distinguished, really, than what goes on in some operating rooms or classrooms—are elevated to unrealistic levels. That's why I believe in humility. Sure, when I went out on the field, I was a so-called star, but when I came off, I tried to be just like everyone else leaving his or her job. I wanted to go home to my family and kids.

Humility is one of the main reasons I sympathize with fans who boo or cheer. To me, by virtue of their admission ticket, they have an inalienable right to let off steam, to derive some satisfaction from sport. And if writing my name on a piece of paper was going to make some youngster look up to me or bring a smile to someone's face, then I was going to do it. And keep on doing it until folks stop asking.

Finally, in the preceding chapter I touched upon some of the finest hitters in the game today. But I would be remiss if I didn't include players like Tony Oliva and Frank Robinson on my all-time hitter list. Oliva could do so much with the bat; he played in pain, he showed me the meaning of the word "pro." Robbie too. After seeing Frank come over from the National League, watching how he went about his job, full-tilt, giving himself up when the situation called for it, you couldn't help but be impressed. Here was a textbook player, a future Hall of Famer, doing whatever it took to win. I should also add Reggie Jackson to this list. Reggie's drive, his intensity, and the impact he had on a team and a game are second to none.

And what about the toughest pitchers I've ever faced? Well, you know about Rudy May. Over the years, Ron Guidry of the Yankees had also been very tough on me. He's left-handed, threw hard, could spot a wicked slider and is very smart. But Ron had been tough on everybody. There are several other pitchers I've gained great respect for over the years—Catfish Hunter, Jim Palmer, and Denny McLain among them. They all shared the same strengths: they didn't beat themselves, always came right after you, didn't walk many guys, and kept the ball in play, relying on the excellent athletes playing behind them.

In closing, I know some of you might be wondering what I'm like off the field. Well, I'm a loving husband, a devoted dad, and a photography buff in my spare time. I'm also a firm believer in putting something back into the game that's willed me so much. I spend a lot of time doing charity and community work, putting on clinics, or just helping some organization that can benefit from my name. But basically I just try to be Rod Carew, the person, whether it's sitting around the house, enjoying the company of my family, watching TV or a movie, or playing a little golf, anything to unwind.

Legendary baseball executive Branch Rickey once said, "Luck is what happens when preparation meets opportunity." Work hard in school, put in your time on the field, and take care of your body—who knows, with a good bounce of the ball here or there, we may someday meet on the steps of Cooperstown.

At this point, I sincerely hope you understand me a little more and certainly my philosophies about hitting. Writing this book has been an enjoyable—and educational—experience. I hope some of my ideas help and you'll begin to improve both your physical and mental approach to the game. I've always wanted to pass along something that, in part, God gave me the ability and desire to do. I hope in some real way this book helps transfer some of that ability and desire to your game. Good luck, work hard, and happy hitting!

Appendix

Rod Carew's Career Highlights

- Sixteenth man in major league history to reach 3,000 career hits, on August 4, 1985

- Seven-time American League batting champion

- 1977 American League Most Valuable Player

- Eighteen-time American League all-star

- Batted over .300 15 years in a row

- Batted .388 in 1977 with 239 hits

- Batted .344 for the decade 1970–79

Major Career Statistics—Rodney Cline Carew (Rod)
Born October 1, 1945, in Gatun, Panama
Throws right- and bats left-handed

Year	Team	Position	G	AB	R	H	2B	3B	HR
1967	Twins	2B	137	514	66	150	22	7	8
1968	Twins	2B-SS	127	461	46	126	27	2	1
1969	Twins	2B	123	458	79	152	30	4	8
1970	Twins	2B-1B	51	191	27	70	12	3	4
1971	Twins	1B-3B	147	577	88	177	16	10	2
1972	Twins	2B	142	535	61	170	21	6	0
1973	Twins	2B	149	580	98	203	30	11	6
1974	Twins	2B	153	599	86	218	30	5	3
1975	Twins	2B-1B	143	535	89	192	24	4	14
1976	Twins	1B-2B	156	605	97	200	29	12	9
1977	Twins	1B-2B	155	616	128	239	38	16	14
1978	Twins	1B	152	564	85	188	26	10	5
1979	Angels	1B	110	409	78	130	15	3	3
1980	Angels	1B	144	540	74	179	34	7	3
1981	Angels	1B	93	364	57	111	17	1	2
1982	Angels	1B	138	523	88	167	25	5	3
1983	Angels	1B-2B	129	472	66	160	24	2	2
1984	Angels	1B	93	329	42	97	8	1	3
1985	Angels	1B	127	443	69	124	17	3	2
Career Totals			G	AB	R	H	2B	3B	HR
19 Seasons			2469	9315	1424	3053	445	112	92

- .328 career batting average in 19 seasons
- Surpassed 200 hits in a season four times
- Currently 23rd on the all-time major league hit list
- Ranks seventh in career one-base hits
- Has 896 career multiple-hit games (two hits or more), including 51 four-hit games
- Hit for cycle (single, double, triple, and home run in one game) June 20, 1970
- Drove in 100 runs in 1977
- Has five career grand-slam home runs
- Stole 49 bases in 1976
- Stole home 17 times in his career, including 7 in 1969
- Played in four American League Championship Series

RBI	TB	BB	SO	SB	CS	OBP	SLG	AVG
51	210	37	91	5	9	.341	.409	.292
42	160	26	71	12	4	.312	.347	.273
56	214	37	72	19	8	.386	.467	.332
28	100	11	28	4	6	.407	.524	.366
48	219	45	81	6	7	.356	.380	.307
51	203	43	60	12	6	.369	.379	.318
62	273	62	55	41	16	.411	.471	.350
55	267	74	49	38	16	.433	.446	.364
80	266	64	40	35	9	.421	.497	.359
90	280	67	52	49	22	.395	.463	.331
100	351	69	55	23	13	.449	.570	.388
70	249	78	62	27	7	.411	.441	.333
44	160	73	46	18	8	.419	.391	.318
59	236	59	38	23	15	.396	.437	.331
21	136	45	45	16	9	.380	.374	.305
44	211	67	49	10	17	.396	.403	.319
44	194	57	48	6	7	.409	.411	.339
31	116	40	39	4	3	.637	.353	.295
39	153	64	47	5	5	.371	.345	.280
RBI	TB	BB	SO	SB	CS	OBP	SLG	AVG
1015	3998	1018	1028	353	187	.393	.429	.328

Acknowledgments

Over the years, many people have played an important role in my career. It is impossible to acknowledge all of you, but you know who you are, and I thank you.

I'd especially like to acknowledge the following:

> *Tony Oliva*, for all his help in my development as a hitter and as a person;
> *Dave Garcia,* for his professionalism and friendship;
> *Vern Morgan,* for the time he spent with a young player on the way up;
> *Billy Martin,* who taught me the importance of hitting within myself;
> *Gene Mauch,* for being a constant reminder of what I can do and what I should do;
> My teammates;
> The 32,000,000 baseball fans who voted me an all-star, year in and year out.

A great deal of time and effort has gone into the preparation of this book (twice). Thanks are due to my wife, Rhonda, Jerome Simon, Chuck Verrill, John Ware, V. J. Lovero, Steven De Vore of SyberVision, Russell Athletic, Pony Sports and Leisure, *Sports Illustrated* magazine, Adam Brunner, Reggie Jackson, Don Mattingly, Don Baylor, Wade Boggs, Tony Gwynn, Steve Garvey, Ron Guidry, Dave Smith, Joe Mauer, Minnesota Twins President David St. Peter, Tim Mead of the California Angels, Jacksonville University Baseball, Cheryl Pronchick, Andy Strassberg, Gary Adams of UCLA, Carl Ruhl, Steve Sandoval, Roni Cafferty, Alex Rowinski, Gil Vieira, Diamond Sports, Ike Hampton of the MLB Academy in Compton, Lou Sauritch for the terrific new photos, and Grant Gordon for a wonderful rewrite of this new and improved version of the book.

Index

Page numbers in *italics* denote images.

college football, 26, 138

compromise, 95

concentration, 26, *53*, 55, 56, 93, *94*, 119

conditioning. *See under* health, and baseball success

confidence, 22–23, 88, *89*, 93–95

consistent contact, 11–13

contact zone, 40, *40*, *51*, *77*, *77*, *78*, *82*

choking up. *See under* gripping the bat

Cooperstown, 13, 169, 170, 171, 181

Craig, Roger, 60

D

designated hitting, 118–19

Detroit Tigers, 22, 28

diet. *See under* health, and baseball success

dominant eye, finding, 68, *68*, 71

Downing, Brian, 115

E

Edmonds, Jim, 72

education, *92*, 93

Ellsbury, Jacoby, 111, 112

exercise. *See under* health, and baseball success

F

Farnsworth, Kyle, 114

fear, 16, *18*, 18–19, *19*, 45, 88, 157–58

See also mental preparation

Fenway Park, 112

Fisk, Carlton, 143

flat-hand hitting, 74, *74*, *75*, 76–79, 81–82

G

Gamboa, Panama, 176

Garvey, Steve, 127, 130

Gatun, Panama, 176

goals, 21, 26

Gonzalez, Adrian, 85

Griffey, Ken, Jr., 93

gripping the bat, *33*
  basics, 32–34, 51
  choking up on the bat, 34, 36–37, 124
  flat-hand hitting, 74–79
  hand position, 32–37, *35*, 51, 69, 74–79
  See also stance; swing

Guerrero, Vlad, 84–85

Guidry, Ron, 181

Gwynn, Tony, 13, 26, 29, 68, 83, 85, 154, 155, 157, 169, 172, 175

H

Hall of Fame, 8, 11, 21, 28, 29, 60, 72, 84, 85, 154, 160, 180

Halladay, Roy, 60

Harris, Lenny, 116

health, and baseball success
  conditioning, *25*, 80, 143–47, *144*
  diet, 149, *150*, 151
  drugs, 143–45
  exercises, specific types, 145–47
  hand exercises, 147, *147*, 149
  and hand health, 32–33
  hydration, 151, *151*

pain, injury, fatigue, *135*, 136, 148, *148*
  playing in pain, 148, *148*
  wind sprints, 145–46, *146*
  See also coaching; mental preparation; practice

Hernandez, Keith, 154–55

high school ball, 52, 82, 114, 155

hitting, techniques for
  "10 Keys to Good Hitting," 16
  aggressiveness, 27
  from an open stance, 44, 45
  ball, contact out in front of the plate, 41
  bat, making it look longer, *29*
  "catching the ball" on the bat, 124, 126
  choking up on the bat, 34, 36–37, 124
  distractions, to reduce, *55*
  dominant eye, finding, *68*, 71
  every hitter unique, 13–14
  fastball, gear your game for, 53, *65*
  hand speed, loose hands source of, 35
  head, move down with the pitch, 79–80
  hit the ball where it's pitched, 9, 79, 84–85
  hitting .300, 12
  hitting middle or top half of the ball, 81
  know the opposition, 12, 46–49, 63, 93, 140
  missing pitches, consistently, 78
  plate coverage, 39, 42, *43*, 66
  playing to your strengths, 20–22

remain on same plane as ball, 50, 64, *69*, 74, *78, 83, 86*

"seeing the ball," 52, 58, 79–80, 96

setup position basics, 51

spoiling the pitch, 51, 85, 172

spraying the ball to all fields, 13

sweet spot, on bat, *30, 31,* 79

time-outs, asking for, 49

unselfishness, 10–11

up the middle/opposite field, 45, 48, 61, 82–83, 106, 107, 136, 143

wait longer on a pitch, 56

weight back, 12

weight forward, 12–13

when to swing, 77–79

wrist release in relation to ball and home plate, 78–79

See also bunting; consistent contact; gripping the bat; hitting zone; left-handed vs. right-handed players; mental preparation; pitches; practice; situational hitting; spin, reading; stance; strikes and the strike zone; swing

hitting zone, 15, *35*, 51, 73, 76, 84, *106*

See also hitting, techniques for

Houston Astros, 19

Howard, Ryan, 22, 82

Hunter, Jim "Catfish," 181

infield pop-ups, avoiding, 80–82

J

Jackson, Reggie, 39, 180

Jackson, Ron, 115

Jeter, Derek, 11, 49, 83, 86, 112

Johnson, Randy, 60

Jordan, Michael, 91

K

Kaline, Al, 28

Kansas City Royals, 11, 21

Kearney, Bob, 101–3

Keeler, "Wee" Willie, 36

Killebrew, Harmon, 11, 72

L

Lau, Charley, 11–12

left-handed vs. right-handed players

advancing a runner, 108, 110

and bunting, 122–23, 127–29, 131

curveball, 59–60

fastball, 59

hit-and-run, 112

hitting ball down the middle, 82–83

left vs. right eye dominance, 68, 71

lefty vs. lefty, righty v. righty, 113–14

practice, 140–41, 143

screwball, 61

stance, 64

target area, 107

and videotaping for analysis, 157

See also bunting; consistent contact; hitting, techniques for; pitches; practice; swing

Little League, 78, 82, 160–62

long-ball attitude, 25

Los Angeles Angels of Anaheim, 72, 114

Los Angeles Dodgers, 50, 114

lower body position, 79–80

M

Major League baseball, 13, 26, 46–47, 84, 140

Mantle, Mickey, 32, 120, 127, 130, 143, 175, 179

Martin, Billy, 157

Mattingly, Don, 50, 93, 169, 172–73, 173, 175

Mauch, Gene, 118

Mauer, Joe, 8–9, 21, 85, 157, 166

May, Rudy, 96, 181

Mays, Willie, 176, 179

McLain, Denny, 181

McNally, Dave, 179

McRae, Hal, 116

media, 90

mental preparation, 10–12, 16, *18*, 18–19, *19*, 21–22, 45, 46–49, 63, 90, 92–93, 96, 97, 99, 100–103, 136, 140, 157–58

See also fear; health, and baseball success; hitting, techniques for

Milwaukee Brewers, 22, 115

Minnesota Twins, 8, *9, 11,* 21–22, 91, 119, 179
Minor League baseball, 26
Minute Maid Park, 112
Morneau, Justin, 21–22
Morris, Jack, 60
Murray, Eddie, 143, 169, *174,* 175
Musial, Stan, *51*

N

National League, 50, 106, 121, 172, 180
New York Mets 112, 154, *167*
New York Yankees, 11, 13, 32, 50, 96, 112, 143, 169, 173, 179, 181
and Yankee Stadium, 30, 92, 112, 179

O

Oliva, Tony, 11, 148, 164, *165,* 180
Ortiz, David, 111

P

pain. *See under* health, and baseball success
Palmer, Jim, 181
Petry, Dan, 60
Pettis, Gary, 100, 102, 111
pinch-hitting, 116, 118
Piniella, Lou, 157
pitches
  breaking ball, general, *52,* 79, 85, 119, 131–32
  change-up, 52, 53, 60–62, *61,* 65
  curveball, 39, 41, 42, 44, 53, 54, 59, *59,* 62, 79, 80, 113
fastball, 41, 42, 45, 49, 54, 56, 62, 64, 80, 107, 112, 119, 131
fastball, gear to, 53, *65*
fastball, reading the spin, 53, 58, 58–60, *60,* 62, 65
fastball, split-finger, 60, *60*
fastball, three-quarter motion, 64
hard thrower on mound, coming over top, 64
inside, 76, 77, 79, 83
knowing the pitcher, 12, 46–49, 63, 93, 140
location and hand position, reading, 62
middle, 16, 40, 50, 77, 78, 110, 129
outside, 42, 45, 49, 66, 77, 78–79, 96, 112, 127, 129
over the top, 54, 59, 64
release point and reading the spin, *54,* 54–56, *56, 57,* 58–61, *59, 61,* 62, *63,* 70
screwball, 52, *53, 61, 65,* 143
sinkerball, 49
slider, 45, 53, 56, 59, 60, 80
sliders, *59,* 60, *60*
spoiling the pitch, 50–51, 85, 172
three-quarter release, 59
See also left-handed vs. right-handed players; spin, reading; strikes and the strike zone
Pittsburgh Pirates, 50, 179
practice
  aluminum vs. wood bats in, 31, 138–39
  bunting, 132–33
  conditioning, 143–47, *144*
exercises, specific types, 145–47
hand exercises, 147, *147,* 149
in-season, 138–39
live pitching, *140*
optimum time, 136–38
perfect practice, 24, 25, 116, 135
pre-game, 139–41
preparing for a season, 136, *137*
purpose, 134, *135,* 136
with right and left-handed pitchers, 141
simulate game situations, 139, *139*
soft toss, *142*
swing, 118–19, *135,* 139, *140,* 141, 143, 148
and switch hitting, 141, 143
wind sprints, 145–46, *146*
See also coaching; health, and baseball success; left-handed vs. right-handed players
pressure, internal, 91
Puckett, Kirby, 11
Pujols, Albert, 13–14, 28–29, 166, 167
pulling the ball, 81

R

Reyes, José, 111, 112, 166, 167, *167,* 169
Reynolds, Mark, 22
rhythm, 66, 70
Rickey, Branch, 181
right-handed vs. left-handed players. *See* left-handed vs. right-handed players
Rivera, Mariano, 143
Rizzuto, Phil, 127

About the Authors

One of the greatest hitters in the history of baseball, **Rod Carew** was enshrined in the Baseball Hall of Fame at Cooperstown in 1991. His accomplishments as a player include eighteen all-star selections, seven batting titles, and awards for both Most Valuable Player and Rookie of the Year. Now a renowned hitting instructor, Carew remains involved with Major League Baseball through executive roles with the Minnesota Twins and Los Angeles Angels of Anaheim, and as the commissioner's Special Advisor for International Player Development in Latin America, Europe, and Australia.

Frank Pace is one of television's most prolific producers, with nearly 600 episodes of network TV to his credit, including the Emmy Award-winning *Murphy Brown*, *Suddenly Susan*, and *George Lopez*. Pace also produced the Emmy-winning movie *Babe Ruth*.

Armen Keteyian is the chief investigative correspondent for CBS News and a correspondent for HBO's "Real Sports with Bryant Gumbel." He is the author or coauthor of nine books, including the *New York Times* bestseller *Raw Recruits*.